Nuclear Weapons: A Very Short Introduction

Very Short Introductions available now:

ADVERTISING Winston Fletcher
AFRICAN HISTORY John Parker and
    Richard Rathbone
AGNOSTICISM Robin Le Poidevin
AMERICAN POLITICAL PARTIES AND
    ELECTIONS L. Sandy Maisel
THE AMERICAN PRESIDENCY
    Charles O. Jones
ANARCHISM Colin Ward
ANCIENT EGYPT Ian Shaw
ANCIENT PHILOSOPHY Julia Annas
ANCIENT WARFARE Harry Sidebottom
ANGLICANISM Mark Chapman
THE ANGLO-SAXON AGE John Blair
ANIMAL RIGHTS David DeGrazia
ANTISEMITISM Steven Beller
THE APOCRYPHAL GOSPELS
    Paul Foster
ARCHAEOLOGY Paul Bahn
ARCHITECTURE Andrew Ballantyne
ARISTOCRACY William Doyle
ARISTOTLE Jonathan Barnes
ART HISTORY Dana Arnold
ART THEORY Cynthia Freeland
ATHEISM Julian Baggini
AUGUSTINE Henry Chadwick
AUTISM Uta Frith
BARTHES Jonathan Culler
BESTSELLERS John Sutherland
THE BIBLE John Riches
BIBLICAL ARCHEOLOGY Eric H. Cline
BIOGRAPHY Hermione Lee
THE BLUES Elijah Wald
THE BOOK OF MORMON Terryl Givens
THE BRAIN Michael O'Shea
BRITISH POLITICS Anthony Wright
BUDDHA Michael Carrithers
BUDDHISM Damien Keown
BUDDHIST ETHICS Damien Keown
CAPITALISM James Fulcher
CATHOLICISM Gerald O'Collins
THE CELTS Barry Cunliffe
CHAOS Leonard Smith
CHOICE THEORY Michael Allingham
CHRISTIAN ART Beth Williamson
CHRISTIAN ETHICS D. Stephen Long
CHRISTIANITY Linda Woodhead
CITIZENSHIP Richard Bellamy
CLASSICAL MYTHOLOGY Helen Morales
CLASSICS Mary Beard and John Henderson

CLAUSEWITZ Michael Howard
THE COLD WAR Robert McMahon
COMMUNISM Leslie Holmes
CONSCIOUSNESS Susan Blackmore
CONTEMPORARY ART Julian Stallabrass
CONTINENTAL PHILOSOPHY
    Simon Critchley
COSMOLOGY Peter Coles
THE CRUSADES Christopher Tyerman
CRYPTOGRAPHY Fred Piper and
    Sean Murphy
DADA AND SURREALISM David Hopkins
DARWIN Jonathan Howard
THE DEAD SEA SCROLLS Timothy Lim
DEMOCRACY Bernard Crick
DESCARTES Tom Sorell
DESERTS Nick Middleton
DESIGN John Heskett
DINOSAURS David Norman
DIPLOMACY Joseph M. Siracusa
DOCUMENTARY FILM
    Patricia Aufderheide
DREAMING J. Allan Hobson
DRUGS Leslie Iversen
DRUIDS Barry Cunliffe
THE EARTH Martin Redfern
ECONOMICS Partha Dasgupta
EGYPTIAN MYTH Geraldine Pinch
EIGHTEENTH-CENTURY BRITAIN
    Paul Langford
THE ELEMENTS Philip Ball
EMOTION Dylan Evans
EMPIRE Stephen Howe
ENGELS Terrell Carver
ENGLISH LITERATURE Jonathan Bate
EPIDEMIOLOGY Roldolfo Saracci
ETHICS Simon Blackburn
THE EUROPEAN John Pinder and
    Simon Usherwood
EVOLUTION Brian and Deborah
    Charlesworth
EXISTENTIALISM Thomas Flynn
FASCISM Kevin Passmore
FASHION Rebecca Arnold
FEMINISM Margaret Walters
FILM MUSIC Kathryn Kalinak
THE FIRST WORLD WAR
    Michael Howard
FORENSIC PSYCHOLOGY David Canter
FORENSIC SCIENCE Jim Fraser

For more information visit our web site:
www.oup.co.uk/general/vsi/

Joseph M. Siracusa

NUCLEAR WEAPONS

A Very Short Introduction

OXFORD
UNIVERSITY PRESS

Great Clarendon Street, Oxford OX2 6DP

Oxford University Press is a department of the University of Oxford.
It furthers the University's objective of excellence in research, scholarship,
and education by publishing worldwide in

Oxford New York

Auckland Cape Town Dar es Salaam Hong Kong Karachi
Kuala Lumpur Madrid Melbourne Mexico City Nairobi
New Delhi Shanghai Taipei Toronto

With offices in

Argentina Austria Brazil Chile Czech Republic France Greece
Guatemala Hungary Italy Japan Poland Portugal Singapore
South Korea Switzerland Thailand Turkey Ukraine Vietnam

Oxford is a registered trade mark of Oxford University Press
in the UK and in certain other countries

Published in the United States
by Oxford University Press Inc., New York

© Joseph M. Siracusa 2008

The moral rights of the author have been asserted

Database right Oxford University Press (maker)

First published 2008

British Library Cataloguing in Publication Data

Data available

Library of Congress Cataloging in Publication Data

Data available

ISBN 978-0-19-922954-3

5 7 9 10 8 6 4

Typeset by SPI Publisher Services, Pondicherry, India
Printed in Great Britain by
Ashford Colour Press Ltd, Gosport, Hampshire

For my wife, Candice

Contents

Preface

This book will consider the most important, common, and recurring questions about the development of nuclear weapons and the policies they have generated. The discussion rests on a single premise: the bomb still matters. Nuclear weapons have not been used in anger since Hiroshima and Nagasaki, more than 60 years ago, yet real concerns about their potential use have remained conspicuously present on the global stage. As president Bill Clinton's first Secretary of Defense, Les Aspin, aptly put it: 'The Cold War is over, the Soviet Union is no more. But the post-Cold War world is decidedly not post-nuclear.' For all the effort for nuclear stockpiles to be reduced down to zero, for the foreseeable future, the bomb is here to stay. Gone may be the days when living with the bomb meant, in the words of former Secretary of State Madeleine Albright, 'Each night we knew that within minutes, perhaps through a misunderstanding, our world could end and morning never come', but if the threat of global thermonuclear war has receded, it has not disappeared. For all our efforts, the prospect of a global post-nuclear age has not progressed much further than wishful thinking. In fact, according to a survey of nuclear experts compiled by the US Senate Foreign Relations Committee in 2005, the world faces a 29% probability that there will be a nuclear strike within the next 10 years. Few dispute this consensus.

Nuclear threats remain fundamental to relations between many states and threaten to become more important. The spread of nuclear weapons will likely spawn two potentially calamitous effects. The first is the threat that terrorists will get their hands on nuclear weapons, a threat that has come into stark relief since the events of 9/11. To be sure, the followers of Osama bin Laden have not yet succeeded in initiating a nuclear attack. But, according to nuclear analysts, it's not because they can't. With a small quantity of enriched uranium, a handful of military supplies readily available on the Internet, and a small team of dedicated terrorists, they could potentially assemble a nuclear weapon in a matter of months, and deliver it by air, sea, rail, or road. The impact of such an attack in the heart of New York or London is almost unimaginable.

A second effect of the spread of nuclear weapons will be the proliferation of threats to use them, greatly complicating global security and in many respects harder to undo. As more states join the nuclear club to enhance their prestige or overcome perceived insecurity, they will undergo their own nuclear learning curve, a process for which, as the experience of the nuclear states over the past 60 years has shown, there is no guarantee of success. The likelihood of mishaps along the way is only too real.

When the atomic bomb was unleashed on the mainland of Japan, in August 1945, in the closing stages of World War II, it was immediately apparent that this was not just another efficient weapon (though it was that, too, as the A-bomb proved more efficient than a conventional 1,000-plane raid). In many respects, Hiroshima was not the kind of watershed moment that can only be seen in retrospect. President Harry S. Truman described the event to a startled world as the very 'harnessing of the basic power of the universe'. It was a view widely shared by influential atomic scientists.

Seven years later, in 1952, the United States scaled the nuclear ladder, detonating its first thermonuclear device in the Pacific. 'Mike', as the bomb was designated, exploded with a force 500 times greater than the bomb detonated over Hiroshima, in the process wiping the test island off the map. The H-bomb really changed everything, transforming the very nature of war and peace. Or, as Winston Churchill put it, 'The atomic bomb, with all its terror, did not carry us outside the scope of human control or manageable events, in thought or action, in peace or war. But ... [with] the hydrogen bomb, the entire foundation of human affairs was revolutionized.' Indeed, it was a brave new world.

A sample of statistics from the nuclear age that followed provides a sobering reminder of the scale of the problem. Upwards of 128,000 nuclear weapons have been produced in the past 60 years, of which about 98% were produced by the United States and the former Soviet Union. The nine current members of the nuclear club – the United States, Russia, Great Britain, France, India, Pakistan, China, Israel, and North Korea – still possess about 27,000 operational nuclear weapons between them. At least another 15 countries currently have on hand enough highly enriched uranium for a nuclear weapon.

Within this context, we will look at the science of nuclear weapons and how they differ from conventional weapons; the race to beat Nazi scientists to the bomb; the history of early attempts to control the bomb, through to the Soviet detonation of an atomic device in August 1949; the race to acquire the H-bomb, with its revolutionary implications; the history of nuclear deterrence and arms control, against the backdrop of the changing international landscape, from the Cold War to the present; the prospect and promise of missile defence, from the end of World War II, through Ronald Reagan's dream of shielding the American homeland from a massive Soviet ballistic attack ('Star Wars'), through the current administration's reduced goal of defending against a small number of ballistic missiles (National Missile Defense), launched by a rogue state; and, finally, the threat and implications of nuclear weapons in the so-called 'age of terrorism'.

In the matter of acknowledgements, I should like to record my debt to my friends and colleagues: Manfred Steger for drawing Oxford University Press's *A Very Short Introduction* series to my attention; Latha Menon, OUP's senior commissioning editor, trade science, for her kind invitation to write this book and unfailing encouragement; Richard Dean Burns for his generosity in sharing his knowledge of arms control and disarmament; and David G. Coleman for his trenchant insights into nuclear deterrence and the making of international strategy. At the personal level, this book owes much to the inspiration of my children – Hanna, Tina, and Joseph – who have inherited the troubled world the 20th century left them; and of course to my wife Candice, to whom this book is dedicated. Needless to say – but I shall say it anyway – I alone am responsible for any errors.

Professor Joseph M. Siracusa
Director of Global Studies
Royal Melbourne Institute of Technology
Melbourne, Australia

List of illustrations

Chapter 1
What are nuclear weapons?

In 1951, the newly established US Federal Civil Defense
Administration (FCDA) commissioned production of a film to
instruct children how to react in the event of a nuclear attack. The
result was *Duck and Cover*, a film lasting nine minutes that was
shown in schools throughout the United States during the 1950s
and beyond. It featured a cartoon character, Bert the Turtle, who
'was very alert' and 'knew just what to do: duck and cover'. At
the sound of an alarm or the flash of a brilliant light signalling a
nuclear explosion, Bert would instantly tuck his body under his
shell. It looked simple enough. And everyone loved the turtle.

Other FCDA initiatives of the early 1950s led to the creation of
the Emergency Broadcast System, food stockpiles, civil defence
classes, and public and private bomb shelters. The FCDA
commissioned other civil defence films, but *Duck and Cover*
became the most famous of the genre. In 2004, the US Library
of Congress even included it in the National Film Registry of
'culturally, historically or aesthetically' significant motion pictures,
a distinction it now shares with such feature-film classics as
Birth of a Nation, *Casablanca*, and *Schindler's List*. As I look
back at the time I was first introduced to Bert the Turtle, in the
early 1950s, while attending primary school on the north side
of Chicago – America's third largest city and long a favourite
hypothetical nuclear target – I realize of course that Bert the

1

Turtle had little to do with culture, history, or aesthetics and much to do with propaganda. America's schoolchildren would never have known what hit them.

The science of nuclear weapons

Atomic energy is the source of power for both nuclear reactors and nuclear weapons. This energy derives from the splitting (fission) or joining (fusion) of atoms. To understand the source of this energy, one must first appreciate the complexities of the atom itself.

An atom is the smallest particle of an element that has the properties characterizing that element. Knowledge about the nature of the atom grew slowly until the early 1900s. One of the first breakthroughs was achieved by Sir Ernest Rutherford in 1911 when he established that the mass of the atom is concentrated in its nucleus; he also proposed that the nucleus has a positive charge and is surrounded by negatively charged electrons. This theory of atomic structure was complemented several years later by Danish physicist Niels Bohr, who placed the electrons in definite shells or quantum levels. Thus an atom is a complex arrangement of negatively charged electrons located in defined shells about a positively charged nucleus. The nucleus, in turn, contains most of the atom's mass and is composed of protons and neutrons (except for common hydrogen, which has only one proton). All atoms are roughly the same size.

Furthermore, the negatively charged electrons follow a random pattern within defined energy shells around the nucleus. Most properties of atoms are based on the number and arrangement of their electrons. One of the two types of particles found in the nucleus is the proton, a positively charged particle. The proton's charge is equal but opposite to the negative charge of the electron. The number of protons in the nucleus of an atom determines what kind of chemical element it is. The neutron is the other type of

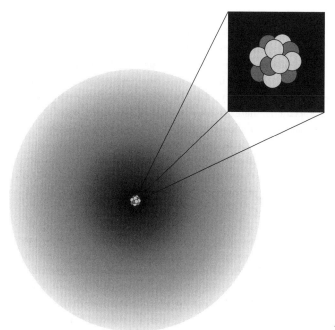

1. An atom consists of electrons, protons, and neutrons. The protons and neutrons make up the dense atomic nucleus whilst the electrons form a more dispersed electron cloud surrounding the nucleus

particle found in the nucleus. Discovered by British physicist Sir James Chadwick, in 1932, the neutron carries no electrical charge and has the same mass as the proton. With a lack of electrical charge, the neutron is not repelled by the cloud of electrons or by the nucleus, making it a useful tool for probing the structure of the atom. Even the individual protons and neutrons have internal structures, called quarks, but these subatomic particles cannot be freed and studied in isolation.

A major characteristic of an atom is its atomic number, which is defined as the number of protons. The chemical properties of an atom are determined by its atomic number. The total number of what is called nucleons (protons and neutrons) in an atom is the atomic mass number. Atoms with the same atomic number but with different numbers of neutrons and, therefore, different atomic masses are called isotopes. Isotopes have identical chemical properties, yet have very different nuclear properties. For example, there are three isotopes of hydrogen: two of these are stable (not radioactive), but tritium (one proton and two neutrons) is unstable. Most elements have stable isotopes. Radioactive isotopes can also be treated for many elements. The nucleus of the U-235 atom (the chemical sign for uranium is U) comprises 92 protons and 143 neutrons (92 + 143 = 235) and is thus written U^{235}.

The mass of the nucleus is about 1% smaller than the mass of its individual protons and neutrons. This difference is called the *mass defect*, and arises from the energy released when the nucleons (protons and neutrons) bind together to form the nucleus. This energy is called *binding energy*, which in turn determines which nuclei are stable and how much energy is released in a nuclear reaction. Very heavy nuclei and very light nuclei have low binding energies; this implies that a heavy nucleus will release energy when it splits apart (fission) and two light nuclei will release energy when they join (fusion). The mass defect and binding energy are famously related to Albert Einstein's $E = mc^2$.

In 1905, Einstein developed the special theory of relativity, one of the implications of which was that matter and energy are interchangeable with one another. This equation states that a mass (m) can be converted into a tremendous amount of energy (E), where c is the speed of light. Because the speed of light is a large number (186,00 miles a second) and thus c squared is huge, a small amount of matter can be converted into a tremendous amount of energy. Einstein's equation is the key to the power of nuclear weapons and nuclear reactors. Fission reaction was used in the first atomic bomb and is still used in nuclear reactors, while fusion reaction became important in thermonuclear weapons and in nuclear reactor development.

What is the practical significance of a nuclear weapon, then? And how does it differ from what came before? The fundamental difference between a nuclear and conventional weapon is, simply put, that nuclear explosions can be many thousands (or millions) of times more powerful than the largest conventional explosion. To be certain, both types of weapons rely on the destructive force of the blast or shockwave. However, the temperatures reached in a nuclear explosion are very much higher than in a conventional explosion, and a large proportion of the energy in a nuclear explosion is emitted in the form of light and heat, generally referred to as thermal energy. This energy is capable of causing severe skin burns and of starting fires at considerable distances; in fact, damage from the resulting firestorm could be far more devastating than the well-known blast effects.

Nuclear explosions are also accompanied by radioactive fallout, lasting a few seconds, and remaining dangerous over an extended period of time, potentially lasting years. The release of radiation is, in fact, unique to nuclear explosions. Approximately 85% of a nuclear weapon produces air blast (and shock) and thermal energy (heat). The remaining 15% of the energy is released as various types of radiation. Of this, 5% constitutes the initial nuclear radiation, defined as that produced within a minute or so of the explosion, and consisting mostly of powerful gamma rays. The final 10% of the total fission energy represents that of the residual (or delayed) nuclear radiation. This is largely due to the radioactivity of the fission products present in the weapon residues, or debris, and fallout after the explosion.

Equally important is the amount of explosive energy that a nuclear weapon can produce, usually measured as the *yield*. The yield is given in terms of the quantity of conventional explosives or TNT that would generate the same amount of energy when it explodes. Thus, a 1 kiloton nuclear weapon is one that produces the same amount of energy in an explosion as does 1,000 tons of TNT; similarly, a 1 megaton weapon would have the energy equivalent of 1 million tons of TNT.

The uranium-based weapon that destroyed Hiroshima in August 1945, the energy of which resulted from splitting (fission) of atoms, had the explosive force of 20,000 tons of TNT; the thermonuclear or hydrogen bomb tested by the United States in the Pacific in October 1952, the energy of which came from joining (fusing) of atoms, had a yield estimated at 7 megatons or 7 million tons of TNT and the production of lethal radioactive fallout from gamma rays. This thermonuclear test was matched by the Soviet Union in August 1953, launching the Cold War superpowers into a deadly race up the nuclear ladder that lasted until the demise of the Soviet Union in December 1991.

Unfortunately, the peaceful end of the Cold War did not mean the end of nuclear threats to global security. Or, to quote former British Prime Minister Tony Blair's defence of his government's plan to update and replace the United Kingdom's Trident nuclear weapons system (see Chapter 7): 'there is also a new and potentially hazardous threat from states such as North Korea which claims already to have developed nuclear weapons or Iran which is in breach of its non-proliferation duties', not to mention the 'possible connection between some of those states and international terrorism'. Add to this stateless terrorist organizations bent on acquiring the means of mass murder and black-market networks of renegade suppliers only too willing to deal in the materials and technical expertise that lead to nuclear weapons, and the picture becomes clearer. The ensuing nightmare of responding to the humanitarian, law and order, and logistical challenges of a nuclear detonation could materialize quite unexpectedly and spectacularly, in any large city, paling the experience of 9/11.

New York City scenario

For example, a relatively small nuclear weapon – say, in the order of a 150 kiloton bomb – constructed by terrorists, detonated in the heart of Manhattan, at the foot of the Empire State Building, at noon on a clear spring day, would have catastrophic consequences. At the end of the first second, the shockwave, causing a sudden change in ambient pressure of 20 pounds per square inch (psi) at a distance of four-tenths of a mile from ground zero, would have destroyed the great landmarks of Manhattan, including the Empire State Building, Madison Square Gardens, Penn Central Railroad Station, and the incomparable New York Public Library. Most of the material that comprises these buildings would remain and pile up to the depth of hundreds of feet in places, but nothing inside this ring would be recognizable. Those caught outside the circle would be exposed to the full effects of the blast, including severe lung and ear drum damage, as well as exposure to flying debris. Those in the direct line of sight of the blast would be exposed to the thermal pulse and killed instantly, while those shielded from some of the blast and thermal effects would be killed as buildings collapse: roughly 75,000 New Yorkers would be killed in these ways. During the next 15 seconds, the blast and firestorm would extend out for almost 4 miles, resulting in 750,000 additional fatalities and nearly 900,000 injuries. And this would just be the beginning of New York's problems.

The task of caring for the injured would literally be beyond the ability, and perhaps even the imagination, of the medical system to respond. All but one of Manhattan's large hospitals lie inside the blast area and would be completely destroyed. There aren't enough available hospital beds in all of New York and New Jersey for even the most critically wounded. The entire country has a total of only 3,000 beds in burn centres; thousands would die from lack of medical attention. Meanwhile, most of New York would be without electricity, gas, water, or sewage. Transportation of the injured and the ability to bring in necessary supplies, people, and equipment would be problematical. Tens of thousands of New Yorkers would be homeless. The tasks of the emergency responders, in areas that remained dangerously radioactive, would pose possibly insuperable problems.

The terrorists' explosion would have produced much more early radioactive fallout than a similar-sized air burst in which the fireball never touches the ground. This is because a surface explosion produces radioactive particles from the ground as well as from the weapon. The early fallout would drift back to earth on the prevailing wind, creating an elliptical pattern stretching from ground zero out into Long Island. Because the wind would be relatively light, the fallout would be concentrated in the area of Manhattan, just to the east of the blast. Thousands of New Yorkers would suffer serious radiation sickness effects, including chromosomal damage, marrow and intestine destruction, and haemorrhaging. Many would die of these conditions in the days and the weeks ahead. Each survivor of the blast would have on average about a 20% chance of dying of cancer of some form, and another 80% probability of dying instead from other causes such as heart disease or infection. The impact on the next generation would come in the form of hereditary illness and birth defects.

In January 2007, the scientists who tend to the Doomsday Clock moved it two minutes closer to midnight, the ultimate symbol of the annihilation of civilization. The *Bulletin of the Atomic Scientists*, which created the clock in 1947 to warn of the dangers of nuclear weapons, advanced the clock to five minutes to midnight. 'We stand at the brink of a second nuclear age', the group said in a statement, pointing to North Korea's first test of a nuclear weapon in 2006, Iran's nuclear ambitions, US flirtation with atomic 'bunker busters', and the 27,000 operational nuclear weapons available to the nuclear club. The scientists also reminded us that only 50 of today's nuclear weapons could kill as many as 200 million people.

Since it was set to seven minutes to midnight in 1947, the hand of the Doomsday Clock has moved 18 times. It came closest to midnight – two minutes away – not surprisingly, in early 1953, following the successful test of America's hydrogen bomb, code-named 'Mike', which somehow managed to vaporize the Pacific island test site. This was about the same time that I was first introduced to Bert the Turtle and his sombre warning, 'duck and cover'. Little has changed.

Chapter 2
Building the bomb

Since late 1944, American long-range B-29 bombers had been conducting the greatest air offensive in history. In total, approximately 160,000 tons of bombs were dropped upon Japan towards the end of the war, including fire-bomb raids that destroyed downtown Tokyo and a number of other large Japanese cities. These raids alone killed 333,000 Japanese soldiers and civilians and wounded half a million more.

Massive loss of life and property in this manner was not unprecedented. Up until the Nazi surrender in May 1945, 635,000 Germans, mostly civilian, died and 7.5 million were made homeless when British and US bombs were dropped on 131 cities and towns. The rationale was simple enough. 'The idea is', observes German revisionist Jorg Friedrich, in his study of Allied bombing of Germany during World War II, 'that the cities and their production and their morale contributed to warfare. So warfare is not simply the business of an army, it's the business of a nation.' In total war, everything and everyone becomes a target. This of course was not news to contemporaries such as George Orwell, who reminds us in the great essay 'England Your England', written in February 1941, with the Luftwaffe overhead: 'highly civilized beings are flying overhead, trying to kill me'.

It was now the turn of Hitler's allies. The Japanese war economy was all but destroyed. But still Japan refused to surrender. Although there were elements within the Japanese government that had long recognized that the war was lost, official Allied policy continued to be nothing less than unconditional surrender. So, while Japanese civilian leaders and Emperor Hirohito favoured suing for peace, the militarists, led by the army, resisted. Faced with such determined resistance, the US Chiefs of Staff estimated that the human costs of invading the Japanese home islands would be no fewer than one million US and Allied casualties. Deeply troubled by such a prospect, President Harry S. Truman, who had succeeded to the presidency after the sudden death of Franklin D. Roosevelt on 12 April 1945, sought alternatives.

For his part, Secretary of War Henry L. Stimson eagerly instructed President Truman on the implications of the potentially devastating new weapon being developed at the top-secret Manhattan Project. On 23 April, Stimson and General Leslie Groves, the project director, gave the new president a lengthy briefing on the weapon we now know as the atomic bomb. Here Groves reported on the genesis and current status of the atomic bomb project, while Stimson presented a memorandum explaining the implication of the bomb for international relations. Stimson addressed the terrifying power of the new weapon, advising that 'within four months, we shall in all probability have completed the most terrible weapon ever known in human history, one bomb which could destroy a whole city'. He went on to allude to the dangers that its discovery and development foreshadowed and pointed to the difficulty in constructing a realistic system of controls.

Truman seemed to focus less on the geopolitical implications of the possession of the atomic bomb and more on the personal burden of having to authorize the use of the awesome weapon.

'I am going to have to make a decision which no man in history has ever had to make', he reportedly said to a White House staffer, the very next person he saw after Stimson and Groves left his office. 'I will make the decision, but it is terrifying to think about what I will have to decide.' In time, Truman would make a choice, probably with insufficient forethought, based on his own wartime experience and information at hand.

Origins of the Manhattan Project

Though no single decision created the American atomic bomb project, most accounts begin with the presidential discussion of a letter written by the most famous scientist of the 20th century, Albert Einstein. On 11 October 1939, Alexander Sachs, Wall Street economist and unofficial advisor to President Franklin D. Roosevelt, met with the president to discuss a letter written by Einstein on 2 August. Einstein had written to inform Roosevelt that recent research had made it 'probable ... that it may become possible to set up a nuclear chain reaction in a large mass of uranium, by which vast amounts of power and large quantities of new radium-like elements could be generated', leading 'to the construction of bombs, and it is conceivable – though much less certain – that extremely powerful bombs of a new type may thus be constructed'. This was all likely to happen 'in the immediate future'.

Einstein believed, rightly, that the Nazi government was actively supporting research in the area and urged the US government to do the same. Sachs read from a cover letter he had prepared and briefed FDR on the main points contained in Einstein's letter. Initially, the president was noncommittal and expressed concern over the necessary funds, but at a second meeting over breakfast the next morning, Roosevelt became persuaded of the value of exploring atomic energy. He could hardly do otherwise.

Einstein drafted his famous letter with the help of Hungarian émigré Leó Szilárd, one of a number of brilliant European physicists who had fled to America in the 1930s to escape Nazi and Fascist repression. Szilárd was among the most vocal of those advocating a programme to develop bombs based on recent findings in nuclear physics and chemistry. Those like Szilárd, and fellow Hungarian refugee physicists Edward Teller and Eugene Wigner, regarded it as their ethical responsibility to alert America to the possibility that German scientists might win the race to build an atomic bomb and to warn that Hitler would be more than willing to resort to such a weapon. But FDR, preoccupied with events in Europe, took over two months to meet with Sachs after receiving Einstein's warning. Szilárd and his colleagues had initially interpreted Roosevelt's apparent inaction as unwelcome evidence that the Americans did not take the threat of nuclear warfare seriously. They were wrong.

Roosevelt wrote back to Einstein on 19 October 1939, informing the physicist that he had set up an exploratory committee consisting of Sachs and representatives of the army and navy to study uranium. Events proved that the president was a man of considerable action once he had chosen a course of direction. In fact, Roosevelt's approval of uranium research in October 1939, based on his belief that the United States could not take the risk of allowing Hitler to achieve unilateral possession of 'extremely powerful Bombs', was the first of many decisions that ultimately led to the establishment of the only atomic bomb effort that succeeded in World War II.

By the beginning of World War II, there was growing concern among scientists in the Allied nations that Nazi Germany might be well on its way to developing fission-based weapons. Organized research first began in Britain as part of the Tube Alloys project, and in America a small amount of funding was given for research into uranium weapons, starting in 1939 with the Uranium

Committee under the direction of Lyman J. Briggs. At the urging of British scientists, though, who made crucial calculations indicating that a fission weapon could be completed in only a few years, by 1941 the project had been wrestled into better bureaucratic hands, and in 1942 came under the auspices of the Manhattan Project. The project brought together the top scientific minds of the day, including many exiles from Nazi Europe, with the production power of American industry, for the single purpose of producing fission-based explosive devices before the Germans. London and Washington agreed to pool their resources and information, but the other Allied partner – the Soviet Union under Joseph Stalin – was not informed.

Berlin, Tokyo, and the bomb

The Allied scientists had much to fear from Berlin. Late in 1938, Lise Meitner, Otto Hahn, and Fritz Strassman discovered the phenomenon of atomic fission. Meitner worked in Germany with physicists Hahn and Strassman until fleeing to Sweden to escape Nazi persecution. From her work in Germany, Meitner knew the nucleus of uranium-235 splits (fission) into two lighter nuclei when bombarded by a neutron, and that the sum of the particles derived from fission is not equal in mass to the original nucleus. Moreover, Meitner speculated that the release of energy – energy a hundred million times greater than normally released in the chemical reaction between two atoms – accounted for the difference. In January 1939, her nephew, the physicist Otto Frisch, substantiated these results and, together with Meitner, calculated the unprecedented amount of energy released. Frisch applied the term 'fission', from biological cell division, to name the process. Danish physicist Niels Bohr sailed for the US shortly thereafter and announced the discovery. In August, Bohr and John A. Wheeler, working at Princeton University, published their theory that the isotope uranium-235, present in trace quantities within uranium-238, was more fissile than uranium-238 and should become the focus of uranium research. They also postulated that a then unnamed, unobserved transuranic element, aptly referred to as 'high octane', produced during fissioning of uranium-238, would be highly fissionable. Enrico Fermi and Leó Szilárd quickly realized the first split or fission could cause a second, and so in a series of chain reactions, expanding in geometric progression. This was the moment Szilárd and fellow atomic scientists persuaded Einstein to write to Roosevelt.

Physicists everywhere soon recognized that if the chain reaction could be tamed, fission could lead to a promising new source of power. What was needed was a substance that could 'moderate' the energy of neutrons emitted in radioactive decay, so that they could be captured by other fissionable nuclei, with heavy water a prime candidate for the job. After the discovery of fission, German Nobel Prize Laureate Werner Heisenberg was recruited to work on a chain-reacting pile in September 1939 by Nazi physicist Kurt Diebner. While the Americans under Fermi chose graphite to slow down or moderate the neutrons produced by the fission in uranium-235 so that they could cause further fissions in a chain reaction, Heisenberg chose heavy water. Heisenberg calculated the critical mass for a bomb in a 6 December 1939 report for the German Arms Weapons Department. His formula, with the nuclear parameters value assumed at that time, yielded a critical mass in the hundreds of tons of 'nearly' pure uranium-235 required for an exploding reaction, Heisenberg's model for a bomb at the time. This was vastly beyond what Germany could hope to produce. With uranium out of the question, the Germans opted for plutonium, which meant building an atomic pile or nuclear reactor to convert natural uranium into plutonium. Unlike America's Manhattan Project, the Nazi nuclear physics programme was never able to produce a critical nuclear reactor, despite the efforts of Heisenberg and Diebner. The Nazi attempt to build a reactor, in fact, proved feeble and disorganized, while their effort to build an atomic weapon was non-existent. But the Allies did not know that. Nor did they know much about Japan's efforts to create a nuclear weapon.

In Tokyo, in autumn 1940, the Japanese army concluded that constructing an atomic bomb was indeed feasible. The Institute of Physical and Chemical Research, or Rikken, was assigned the project under the direction of Yoshio Nishina. The Imperial Navy was also diligently working to create its own 'superbomb' under a project dubbed F-Go (or No. F, for fission), headed by Bunsaku Arakatsu, towards the end of 1945. The F-Go programme had begun life at Kyoto in 1942. However, the military commitment wasn't backed with adequate resources, and the Japanese effort to build an atomic bomb had made little progress by the end of the war.

Japan's nuclear efforts were disrupted in April 1945 when a B-29 raid damaged Nishina's thermal diffusion separation apparatus. Some reports claim the Japanese subsequently moved their atomic operations to Hungnam, now part of North Korea. The Japanese may have used this facility for making small quantities of heavy water. The Japanese plant was captured by Soviet troops at war's end, and some reports claim that the output of the Hungnam plant was collected every other month by Soviet submarines, as part of Moscow's own nuclear energy programme (see Chapter 4).

There are indications that Japan had a more sizeable programme than is commonly understood, and that there was close cooperation among the Axis powers, including the secretive exchange of war materiel. The Nazi submarine U-234, which surrendered to American forces in May 1945, was found to be carrying 560 kilograms of uranium oxide destined for Japan's own atomic programme. The oxide contained about 3.5 kilograms of the isotope U-235, which would have been one-fifth of the total U-235 needed to make one bomb. After Japan surrendered in August 1945, the occupying US army found five Japanese cyclotrons, which could be used to separate fissional material from ordinary uranium. The Americans smashed the cyclotrons and dumped them into Tokyo harbour.

The road to Trinity

A massive industrial and scientific undertaking, employing
65,000 workers, the Manhattan Project involved many of
the world's great physicists in the scientific and development
aspects. For its part, the United States made an unprecedented
investment into wartime research for the project, which was
spread over 30 sites in the US and Canada. The actual design
and construction of the weapon was centralized at a secret
laboratory in Los Alamos, Mexico, previously a small ranch
school near Santa Fe. The laboratory that designed and fabricated
the first atomic bombs began to take shape in spring 1942
with the recommendation that the US Office of Scientific and
Research Development and the army look at ways to further
bomb development. By the time of his appointment in late
September, General Groves had orders to set up a committee
to study military applications of the bomb. Shortly thereafter,
J. Robert Oppenheimer headed the work of a group of theoretical
physicists he called the luminaries, which included Felix Bloch,
Hans Bethe, Edward Teller, and Robert Seber, while John H.
Manley assisted him by coordinating nationwide fission research
and instrument and measurement studies from the Metallurgical
Laboratory in Chicago. Despite inconsistent experimental results,
the consensus emerging at Berkeley (from where most of the
scientists had been seconded) was that approximately twice as
much fissionable material would be required than had been
estimated six months earlier. This was disturbing, especially in
light of the military's view that it would take more than one bomb
to win the war.

In many ways, the Manhattan Project operated like any other
large construction company. It purchased and prepared sites,
let contracts, hired personnel and subcontractors, built and
maintained housing and service facilities, placed orders for
materials, developed administrative and accounting procedures,
and established communications networks. By the end of the war,

General Groves and his staff had spent approximately $2.2 billion on, among other things, production facilities and towns in the states of Tennessee, Washington, and New Mexico, as well as on research in university laboratories from Columbia University, in New York City, to the University of California at Berkeley. What made the Manhattan Project clearly unlike other companies performing similar functions was that, because of the necessity of moving quickly, it invested hundreds of millions of dollars in unproven and hitherto unknown processes, and did so entirely in secret. Speed and secrecy were the watchwords of the Manhattan Project.

Secrecy proved to be a blessing in disguise. Although it dictated remote site locations, required subterfuge in obtaining labour and supplies, and served as a constant irritant to the academic scientists on the project, it had one overwhelming advantage: secrecy made it possible to make decisions with little regard for normal peacetime considerations. Groves knew that as long as he had the backing of the president, money would be available and he could devote his energies entirely to the running of the project. Secrecy was so complete that many of the staff did not know what they were working on until they heard about the bombing of Hiroshima on the radio.

Moreover, the need for haste clarified priorities and shaped decision-making. Unfinished research on three separate, unproven processes had to be used to freeze design plans for production facilities, even though it was recognized that later findings would dictate changes. The pilot stage was eliminated entirely, violating all manufacturing practices and leading to intermittent shutdowns and endless troubleshooting during trial runs in production facilities. The inherent problems of collapsing the stages between the laboratory and full production created an emotionally charged atmosphere, with optimism and despair alternating with confusing frequency.

Despite Groves's assertion that an atomic bomb could probably be produced by 1945, he and other principals associated with the project fully recognized the magnitude of the tasks before them. For any large organization to take laboratory research into design, construction, operation, and product delivery in two and a half years (from 1943 to August 1945) would have been a major industrial achievement. Whether the Manhattan Project would be able to produce bombs in time to affect the outcome of World War II was an altogether different question as 1943 began. And, obvious though it seems in retrospect, it must be remembered that no one at the time knew the war would end in 1945 or, equally important, who the remaining adversaries would be when and if the atomic bomb was ready to use.

At precisely 5:30 a.m., on Monday 16 July 1945, at 'Trinity', the code-name for the Manhattan Project test site in Alamogordo, New Mexico, a group of officials and scientists led by Groves and Oppenheimer witnessed the first explosion of an atomic bomb. And what a show it was. A pinprick of brilliant light punctured the darkness of the New Mexico desert, vaporizing the tower and turning asphalt around the base of the tower to green sand. The bomb released the explosive force of nearly 19,000 tons of TNT, and the New Mexico sky was suddenly brighter than many suns. Some observers suffered temporary blindness even though they looked at the brilliant light through smoked glass. Seconds after the explosion came a huge blast, sending searing heat across the desert and knocking some observers, standing 1,000 yards away, to the ground. A steel container weighing over 200 tons, standing a half-mile from ground zero, was knocked ajar. As the orange and yellow fireball stretched up and spread, a second column, narrower than the first, rose and flattened into a mushroom cloud, providing the atomic age with a symbol that has since become imprinted on the human consciousness. *New York Times* reporter William Laurence called the explosion 'the first cry of a new-born world'.

2. A replica of 'Fat Man'

For a fraction of second, the light produced by Trinity was greater than any ever before produced on earth, and could have been seen from another planet. And as the light dimmed and the mushroom cloud rose, Oppenheimer was reminded of fragments from the *Bhagavad-Gita*, the sacred Hindu text, 'I am become Death/The shatterer of worlds'. Less quoted but more memorable perhaps was the comment by test site manager Kenneth Bainbridge to Oppenheimer: 'Oppie, now we're all sons of bitches.' The terrifying destructive power of atomic weapons and the uses to which they could be put were to haunt many of the Manhattan Project scientists for the remainder of their lives.

By the end of July, the Manhattan Project had produced two different types of atomic bombs, code-named 'Fat Man' and 'Little Boy'. Fat Man was the more complex of the two. A bulbous, 10-foot bomb containing a sphere of metal plutonium-239, it was surrounded by blocks of high explosives that were designed to produce a highly accurate and symmetrical implosion. This would compress the plutonium

3. A replica of 'Little Boy'

sphere to a critical density and set off a nuclear chain reaction. Scientists at Los Alamos were not altogether confident in the plutonium bomb design – hence the necessity of the Trinity test. The Little Boy type of bomb had a much simpler design than Fat Man. Little Boy triggered a nuclear explosion, rather than implosion, by firing one piece of uranium-235 into another. When enough U-235 is brought together, the resulting fission chain reaction can produce a nuclear explosion. But the critical mass must be assembled very quickly; otherwise, the heat released at the start of the reaction will blow the fuel apart before most of it is consumed. To prevent this inefficient pre-detonation, the uranium bomb used a gun to fire one piece of U-235 down the barrel into another. Moreover, the bomb's gun-barrel shape was believed to be so reliable that testing was ruled out. Interestingly, testing would have been out of the question anyway, since producing Little Boy had used all the purified U-235 produced to date. Clearly, though, the Manhattan Project had managed to take the discovery of fission from the laboratory to the battlefield.

The Hiroshima decision

General Groves quickly conveyed word of the test to Secretary of War Stimson's aide, who in turn relayed word to his boss in cryptic fashion: 'Operated on this morning. Diagnosis not yet complete but results seem satisfactory and already exceed expectations.' Stimson, filled with excitement, gave Truman a preliminary report in the evening, after the president returned from his tour of Berlin while still at the Potsdam Conference. While the success of the bomb took a great load off his mind, Truman, up to then uncertain whether he would need Soviet assistance to finish off the Japanese, casually informed Stalin that the US 'had a new weapon of unusual destructive force'. Stalin, who had spies on the ground in New Mexico, simply replied that he hoped he would use it well. Certainly, with the success of 'Trinity', the US government believed that it could probably conclude the war without Russian assistance, and from Potsdam, Truman sent an ultimatum to Tokyo to surrender immediately, unconditionally, or face 'prompt and utter destruction'.

In any case, the US now had in its arsenal a weapon of unparalleled destruction; Stimson even suggested that it would create 'a new relationship of man to the universe'. Truman's advisers agreed that the atomic bomb could end the war in the Pacific, but they could not agree on the best way to use it. There is a certain irony here: the scientists who developed the bomb wanted it used against the Nazis and were horrified when it became clear it would be used against Japan. Some proposed a public demonstration on an uninhabited region; others argued that it should be used against Japanese naval forces and should never be used against Japanese cities. Still others argued that the objective was not so much to defeat Japan as to employ 'atomic diplomacy' against the Soviet Union, providing a demonstration to make it more manageable in Eastern and Central Europe after the war.

After considering the various proposals, Truman concluded that the only way to shorten the war, while avoiding an invasion of Japan, was to use the bomb against Japanese cities. On the morning of 6 August 1945, shortly after 8:15 a.m., a lone B-29 bomber named the *Enola Gay* dropped Little Boy over the city of Hiroshima (population 350,000), Japan's second most important military-industrial centre, instantly killing 80,000 to 140,000 people and seriously injuring 100,000 or more. The first (never before tested) uranium-235-based bomb to be used had the explosive force of 20,000 tons of TNT – puny and primitive by later thermonuclear standards. Still, in that one terrible moment, 60% of Hiroshima, 4 square miles, an area equal to one-eighth of New York City, was destroyed. The burst temperature was estimated to reach over a million degrees Celsius, which ignited the surrounding air, forming a fireball some 840 feet in diameter. Eyewitnesses more than 5 miles away said its brightness exceed the sun tenfold. The blast wave shattered windows for a distance of 10 miles and was felt as far away as 37 miles. Over two-thirds of Hiroshima's buildings were demolished. The hundreds of fires, ignited by the thermal pulse, combined to produce a firestorm that had incinerated everything within about 4.4 miles of ground zero. Hiroshima had disappeared under thick, churning foam of flame and smoke.

Three days later, on 9 August, another lone B-29 bomber, named *Bock's Car*, dropped Fat Man (the Trinity test bomb) on Nagasaki (population 253,000), home to two huge Mitsubishi war plants on the Urakami River, instantly killing 24,000 and wounding 23,000. The plutonium bomb had the explosive force of 22,000 tons of TNT, a force equivalent to the collective load of 4,000 B-29 bombers, or more than 2,000 times the blast power of what had previously been the world's most devastating bomb, the British 'Grand Slam', a logical technological improvement in the strategy of city-busting that the Allies had developed at Hamburg and Dresden. But unlike Hiroshima, there was no firestorm this time. Despite this, the blast was more destructive to the

4. The mushroom cloud rising over Hiroshima

immediate area, due to the topography and greater power of Fat
Man. However, the hilly, almost mountainous terrain limited the
total area of destruction to less than that of Hiroshima, and the
resulting loss of life was also not as great. With Japanese doctors
at a loss to explain why many civilian patients who had not been
wounded were now wasting away, in the following weeks the
death counts in both cities rose as the populations succumbed to
radiation-related sickness.

The shockwaves were felt well beyond the Japanese home islands. Western newspapers struggled to explain to a triumphant but mystified public how thousands of American, British, and Canadian scientists had managed to harness the power of the sun to such deadly effect. No easier to explain was that the US government could undertake a military and scientific programme as massive and prolonged as the Manhattan Project with such absolute secrecy. This paradoxical view of the government's achievement was typical of the American public's response to the bomb. The elation at the prospect of imminent peace was tempered by a growing recognition of the awesome responsibilities of possessing such a powerful weapon. Critics such as British scientist P. M. S. Blackett argued that Hiroshima and Nagasaki could best be seen as the first chapter of the Cold War rather than the last chapter of World War II. Opposition to nuclear energy emerged almost immediately after the bomb was built. The Franck Report of 11 June 1945, signed by a number of the Manhattan Project scientists, warned Secretary of War Stimson that an unannounced attack would surely lead to an arms race. Both the report and the scientists were ignored.

The impact of the new weapon spread well beyond the military and scientific circles in which it had been developed; to an extent unprecedented, it began to seep into the popular imagination as images of mushroom clouds became symbolic of the new destructive potential that had been created. What Truman called 'the greatest scientific gamble in history' had paid off with devastating effectiveness, and there was no doubt that a turning point in the history of the contemporary world had been reached. Indeed, 'the bomb', as it was quickly dubbed, became the defining feature of the post-World War II world.

With a Japanese surrender imminent, and recognizing that if it was going to play a part in post-war Asia it would need to enter the fray quickly, the Soviet Union declared war on Japan on 8 August, a week sooner than Stalin had pledged at the

Potsdam Conference. Nine minutes after its declaration, the Soviet Union's Far Eastern army and air force launched a massive offensive against the Japanese forces in Manchuria and the Korean peninsula. The seizure of the Kurile Islands and southern Sakhalin also constituted part of the Soviet continental campaign. The overwhelming nature of the Soviet attack caused very high casualties among the Kwantung army, killing 80,000 Japanese soldiers (against 8,219 Soviet dead and 22,264 wounded) in less than a week. The writing was on the wall.

Yielding to the reality of the situation, Emperor Hirohito, supported by civilian advisers, finally overcame the militarists and ordered surrender on 14 August. For its part, the United States agreed to retain the institution of the emperor system, stripped of pretension to divinity and subject to American occupation headed by General Douglas MacArthur. On 2 September, thereafter known as V-J Day, a great Allied fleet sailed into Tokyo Bay. Aboard the *USS Missouri*, General MacArthur accepted Japanese surrender on behalf of the Allies. With this simple ceremony, World War II was finally brought to a close.

Chapter 3

'A choice between the quick and the dead'

When we contemplate the origins and issues of nuclear disarmament in the immediate aftermath of World War II, we should bear in mind that at the beginning of the nuclear age, there were no rules, no non-proliferation norms, no concept of nuclear deterrence, and, particularly, no taboo against nuclear war. There was, however, an apparent arms race, hard on the heels of a conflict that probably killed 60 million souls. At the same time, advances in atomic energy held out prospects for important peaceful uses, such as nuclear power providing limitless energy to the world. Significantly, the processes associated with the military and civilian uses of atomic energy were virtually the same.

Traditionally, as with most scientific advances, there were efforts to share information at the international level. But because of the well-known destructive ability of the atomic bomb and the power that it gave its possessor, America was in no mood to share its nuclear secrets in the absence of an effective international control system. Reconciling the drive to reap the peaceful benefits of this newly harnessed force with the need to control its destructive potential was always going to pose a problem.

Early efforts focused on countering the problem with international agreements and tied non-proliferation with disarmament. Not two months had passed since Hiroshima when President Harry S. Truman told Congress that: 'The hope of civilization lies in international arrangements looking, if possible, to the renunciation of the use and development of the atomic bomb.' It was a view widely shared by influential atomic scientists. The Franck Report, named after the chairman of the committee issuing the report, recommended in June 1945, before the atomic bombs were dropped on Japan, that since a perpetual US monopoly would likely be impossible to maintain, the elimination of nuclear weapons would have to be realized through international agreements.

Several political actions occurred that were aimed at establishing a framework in which to consider the control of atomic energy. The Three Nation Agreed Declaration was concluded among the United States, Great Britain, and Canada, wartime partners in the development of the bomb. On 15 November 1945, in Washington, the three countries declared their intent to share with all nations the scientific information associated with atomic energy for peaceful or civilian purposes. Recognizing the dilemma of reconciling the peaceful and destructive powers of atomic energy, the declaration called for withholding this information until appropriate safeguards were in place. It then called on the United Nations to establish a commission to recommend a system of international control.

At the Conference of Ministers meeting, held in Moscow on 27 December 1945, the Soviet Union agreed to these principles in the Moscow Declaration, a Soviet-Anglo-US statement. The declaration also contained the text of a proposed UN resolution to establish a commission on controlling atomic energy; it invited France, China, and Canada to co-sponsor the resolution, which was passed unanimously during the first session of the UN General Assembly, on 24 January 1946.

In this way, the United Nations Atomic Energy Commission (UNAEC) was established. It consisted of all members of the

UN Security Council (Australia, Brazil, China, Egypt, France, Mexico, the Netherlands, Poland, the Soviet Union, the United Kingdom, and the United States), together with Canada – a total of 12 countries. The resolution called for the commission to be accountable to the Security Council, dominated by America, Britain, China, and the Soviet Union. This move, suggested by Moscow, demonstrated how the efforts to share atomic knowledge would be dominated by Security Council considerations. The Security Council also operated with a veto power for each permanent member on substantive but not procedural issues. The veto – then and now – would play an important role in the efforts to control the atom.

The responsibilities of the UNAEC included, among others, overseeing the exchange of basic scientific information for peaceful ends; control of atomic energy to ensure its use for only peaceful ends; the elimination of atomic weapons from national arsenals; and effective safeguards by way of inspection and other means to protect complying states against the hazards of violation and evasion.

At the same time, Secretary of State James F. Byrnes formed a committee to study methods of control and safeguards to protect the United States during the negotiations. The five members of the group, led by Assistant Secretary of State Dean Acheson, were drawn from military and political circles associated with the bomb's development. Acheson's committee looked to a 'Board of Consultants' as a source of knowledge on technical aspects of atomic energy. The board was led by David Lilienthal, Chairman of the Tennessee Valley Authority, and included three other scientists, notably J. Robert Oppenheimer, the physicist who played a major role in the Manhattan Project.

The combined effort of these two groups resulted in a document entitled 'A Report on the International Control of Atomic Energy', which promptly became known as the 'Acheson-Lilienthal

Report'. Released in late March 1946, the report highlighted the technical characteristics that would determine the nature of an international control system. More important, the conferees regarded their conclusions as a foundation for discussion rather than a final plan. The United States proposal at the UNAEC would draw heavily on the Acheson-Lilienthal Report's ideas for a system of international control.

The Baruch Plan

This is the background behind the US proposals made to the United Nations in June 1946. Known as the Baruch Plan after its chief negotiator Bernard Baruch, the elder statesman who had served American presidents in various capacities since World War I, the plan's objective was to prevent the further spread of nuclear weapons, ostensibly by securing atomic technology and materials through the control of the newly created United Nations. Under the plan, a UN authority would supervise and control the mines of the raw materials for atomic weapons and would be responsible for any production. Also, under the plan, the United States would give up its atomic weapons and facilities in a phased transition.

In presenting the plan to the United Nations on 14 June 1946, Baruch employed a melodramatic allusion to America's Wild West past: 'We are here to make a choice between the quick and the Dead. ... If we fail, then we have damned every man to be a slave of Fear. Let us not deceive ourselves: We must elect World Peace or World Destruction.' The fundamentals of the Baruch Plan were easy enough for the public to grasp. The former chairman of Woodrow Wilson's War Industries Board proposed the creation of an International Atomic Development Authority whose sole duty would be to oversee all phases of the development and use of atomic energy; the key to the successful operation of such an agency would be its effectiveness in controlling and inspecting atomic energy activities – for then, and only then would the United States be prepared both to cease the manufacture of atomic weapons and dispose of its stockpile.

Baruch listed several activities that would be regarded as criminal: possession or separation of atomic material suitable for use in a bomb; seizure of property owned or licensed by the authority; interference with the authority's activities; and engaging in 'dangerous' projects that were contrary to, or without a licence by the authority. Then, making his own distinctive contribution, Baruch called for severe penalties to be imposed on countries that engaged in such activities. And although he conceded the importance of the veto power to the work of the Security Council, he said that with respect to atomic energy, 'there must be no veto to protect those who violate their solemn agreement not to develop or use atomic energy for destructive purposes'.

Responses to the plan varied widely. After reading the speech, Winston Churchill praised Baruch, saying, 'There is no man in whose hands I would rather see these awful problems placed than Bernard Baruch's.' Some opposed it for giving too much away; others opposed it as being unfair to the Soviets and called for an immediate halt in the manufacture of atomic bombs. Some 30 senators said the plan was not tenable, while Senate Foreign Relations Committee chairman Arthur Vandenberg said the plan was 'more important to the peace of the world than anything that happened in New York'. By September, one survey reported that 78% of the American public endorsed the plan.

The issue of the veto prompted both favourable and critical comments. The famous columnist Walter Lippmann accused Baruch of taking America up a blind alley with the veto provision, while Supreme Court Justice William O. Douglas supported Baruch's proposal to strip the Security Council of its veto in atomic matters. The American *Daily Worker*, the US Communist Party paper, saw the elimination of the veto as an opportunity for Washington and London to 'carry the day' against the Soviet Union, 'demonstrating a new predatory flight of the American eagle'. The Kremlin's response to the Baruch Plan came five days later, on 19 June, in an address delivered by Soviet deputy foreign minister Andrei Gromyko.

The Gromyko Plan

Sidestepping the American case for atomic peace, Gromyko instead called for an international convention aimed at prohibiting the production and employment of atomic weapons, while demanding unilateral nuclear disarmament by the United States as a precondition for any agreement. To this end, he introduced two resolutions. The first called for the convention to ban the use and production of atomic bombs, destroying existing weapons within three months, while calling on the principals to pass laws within their own countries to punish violators; the second called for the formation of two committees, one for exchanging scientific information and the other to find ways to ensure compliance with the provisions.

The only direct response to the Baruch Plan came in the form of Soviet opposition to eliminating the veto: 'Attempts to undermine the principles, as established by the Charter of the Security Council, including the unanimity of the members of the security council in deciding questions of substance, are incompatible with the interests of the United Nations ... [and] must be rejected.' It was unlikely that Joseph Stalin's representative could have said anything else, as the Cold War lines were being drawn.

Washington's official reaction was low-key. In a press conference, one member of the US delegation said he was not discouraged and characterized the Soviet proposal 'by way of argument rather than a final Soviet position'. In order to avoid an open split at this early stage of negotiations, the American delegation used anonymous stories in the press to make its point. Accordingly, the *New York Times* reported that according to a reliable source, the United States was not able to accept the Gromyko Plan, at least not in the absence of the safeguards proposed by Baruch, as it meant giving up America's source of military power.

Initially, the UNAEC agreed to break up into a working committee of the whole, in order to draft a plan incorporating all of the ideas suggested for the international control authority. Both Washington, noting the level of support for its proposal, and Moscow reiterated their respective positions. After some delay with Gromyko over its name, a smaller group – Subcommittee One – was formed to draft possible features that a control plan might have; the membership of Subcommittee One was composed of France, Mexico, Britain, the United States, and the Soviet Union.

Subcommittee One met on 1 July, a day after the United States had conducted a test of an atomic Bomb at Bikini Atoll, evidence to some that America had no intention of relinquishing its monopoly over the bomb. In addition to handing a propaganda victory to the Soviets, continuing the US tests may have provided the impetus for them to pursue their own. Another test was held on 25 July. In September, however, Truman postponed the next test – scheduled for March 1947 – partly out of deference to the negotiations.

The discussions in Subcommittee One highlighted some of the basic differences between the sides. Gromyko insisted on outlawing atomic weapons first, and was less concerned about a system of control. For their part, the Americans demanded adequate control before they would give up their weapons.

The opposing positions of each country on the veto issue became further entrenched. And although the goal of the Americans in submitting the memoranda had been to elicit more specific responses from the Soviets, Gromyko held his ground.

The chairman of Subcommittee One, Australian external affairs minister Herbert Evatt, recognized the impasse and proposed to the full UNAEC that three committees of the whole be formed to address technical questions, leaving political questions aside, all in the hope of finding common ground. By majority vote, the group formed Committee Two, the Scientific and Technical Committee, the only one whose formation the Soviets supported, and a Legal Committee. The most important work occurred in the Scientific and Technical Committee.

Committee Two met first, but was unable to move beyond the differences experienced in Subcommittee One and became the forum for Gromyko's outright rejection of the Baruch Plan. In sum, he said, on 24 July 1946, 'The United States proposals in their present form cannot be accepted in any way by the Soviet Union either as a whole or in separate parts.' He also refused to yield to the elimination of the veto. Harkening back to the founding of the United Nations, Gromyko underscored the importance of the issue of sovereignty in the deliberations. He addressed the Baruch Plan to consider atomic energy as a matter of international and not of national importance. Accordingly, he viewed this principle as a violation of Article 2, Paragraph 7 of the United Nations Charter, which called for no interference in the internal affairs of member states.

The Scientific and Technical Committee had begun meeting on 19 July 1946, and the framework within which the members operated proved highly successful. Forming an informal group of scientists, the committee agreed that no one in the group would represent his country; the members would simply explore the technical aspects of safeguards as individuals. Whatever conclusions they drew would be referred back to the main committee. The United States provided, in addition to the technical information in the Acheson and Lilienthal Report, background information and information on the beneficial use of atomic energy in 11 different treatises. In response to its mandate, the committee completed its report on 3 September, concluding that it had been unable to find 'any basis in the available scientific facts for supposing that effective control is not technologically feasible'. There was always going to be another problem – the political kind.

As the work of the committee became bogged down, Baruch decided to write a letter to Truman, seeking approval for two recommendations. The first would be to force a vote in the UNAEC at an early date, preferably before January 1947, when the membership of the commission would rotate; the second would be a call for military preparedness in the field of atomic energy, in the likely failure of the UNAEC.

Widespread news coverage of the views of Secretary of Commerce Henry Wallace, who was scathing of the Baruch Plan, provided the backdrop of Baruch's visit to the White House to deliver his letter on 18 September. Wallace's remarks, well received by a liberal audience, had hit Baruch to the quick, badly undercutting him publicly. Wallace said that a major defect of the Baruch Plan was America's insistence that other countries give up their right to explore military uses of nuclear energy and turn over raw materials to an international authority, whereas the United States would not give up its weapons until it deemed such a system was in place. Wallace did not believe the US would be amenable to such a deal if the tables were turned.

To Baruch, such a display of disunity could only undermine the impact of the coming UNAEC vote. At the Paris Peace Conference of Foreign Ministers, Secretary of State James F. Byrnes made a similar complaint, arguing that Wallace's statements had eroded his own position there. Both Baruch and Byrnes threatened to resign if Wallace did not recant. With the writing on the wall, Truman asked for, and received, Wallace's resignation, on 20 September.

As the Wallace-Baruch affair continued in the press, the Soviets finally called for a vote on the Scientific and Technical Committee's report. The group was pleased by the Soviet vote in favour of the report, but the feeling was short-lived. The Soviet representative stated that his vote was accompanied by a reservation, based on the fact that the information on which the report's conclusions were based was incomplete and therefore should be regarded as hypothetical and conditional. Committee Two formally accepted the report of the Scientific and Technical Committee on 2 October and began hearing testimony from various experts in the field.

Although Committee Two was proceeding smoothly, various Soviet actions through October 1946 made it fairly clear that the sides were poles apart. Meanwhile, Baruch pressed Truman for an answer to his September letter that called for an early vote. By the time Baruch received permission in November to force a vote by the end of the year, the Baruch Plan had all but been rejected and his reputation subject to vicious attacks by the Soviets in the UN.

The Cold War steps in

On 13 November, at the first plenary meeting of the United Nations Atomic Energy Commission in four months, the vote was ten in favour, two (USSR and Poland) abstaining, that the UNAEC should report its finding and recommendation to the Security Council by 31 December 1946. Despite Soviet delaying tactics, Baruch moved closer to his goal of an early vote. On 5 December, Baruch, whose position had been reaffirmed by the White House, proposed that the plan bearing his name be adopted as a recommendation to the Security Council, but did not insist on a vote on that day. On 20 December, the UNAEC rejected the Soviet proposal to postpone the vote for a week, while the Polish delegation proposed to refer the Baruch Plan to the Political and Social Committee of the UN General Assembly. At this point, Gromyko simply refused to participate any further, a position he maintained throughout the end of the year.

Several days later, on 26 December, Committee Two passed its report on safeguards and forwarded it to the Working Committee, which the next day discussed the Baruch Plan, one paragraph at a time. There was only one area of disagreement: the veto. The group agreed to report to the full UNAEC, with a cover letter explaining the remaining dispute, and a note that the Soviets had not participated. At the final meeting of the UNAEC, on 30 December, the group agreed to Baruch's proposal to adopt the Working Committee report and submit it to the Security Council the next day. It passed by a majority but without Soviet agreement, producing what future Democratic Senator from Connecticut, Joseph I. Lieberman, called 'a hollow victory' for the United States.

As planned, Baruch resigned shortly after the vote, giving his place to the US representative to the UN, Warren Austin, presumably strengthening the American hand by combining the negotiator and the representative in the same person. The Security Council discussed the report without much success until March 1947, when it passed a resolution to refer discussions back to the UNAEC. The UNAEC provided the second report in September; their deliberations had included 12 Soviet amendments to the first UNAEC report, all of which had been rejected. The Security Council did not consider the second report of the UNAEC, which continued to meet through the spring of 1948. A third UNAEC report concluded that the group had reached an impasse and requested that the Security Council suspend its deliberations. In the summer of 1948, the Soviets vetoed a Security Council resolution approving all the UNAEC reports, while a non-binding resolution of the General Assembly approved the majority plan, hoping that the UNAEC would one day find a way to bring atomic weapons under control. Hope apparently ran out in November 1949 when the General Assembly agreed to suspend the work of the United Nations Atomic Energy Commission.

When Bernard Baruch presented the United States' initial proposal dealing with atomic weapons at the inauguration of the United Nations Atomic Energy Committee in June 1946, he launched the first of what would become hundreds, if not thousands, of multilateral and bilateral discussions on arms control measures during the next six decades. The 'Baruch Plan' would have created an International Atomic Development Authority to control or own all activities associated with atomic energy, from raw materials to military applications, and inspect all other uses. The Soviets and other delegates challenged the US proposal since the Americans did not relinquish their atomic arsenal, while expecting others to forgo developing their own. They were not far off target. 'America can get what she wants if she insists on it', Baruch asserted in December 1946. 'After all, we've got it and they haven't, and won't for a long time to come.' Baruch was wrong on both points: the Soviets rejected his plan and soon produced atomic bombs (see Chapter 4).

'Neither the United States nor the Soviet Union was prepared in 1945 or 1946 to take the risks that the other power required for agreement', historian Barton Bernstein concluded. 'In this sense, the stalemate on atomic energy was a symbol of the mutual distrust in Soviet-American relations.' Washington's continued insistence, beginning with the Baruch Plan, upon intrusive inspection systems to verify treaty compliance, which Moscow viewed as sanctioned espionage, figured prominently in stalemating future arms control endeavours. That it could have been otherwise in 'a struggle for the very soul of mankind', to quote former president George Herbert Walker Bush, in a different but related context many years later, should not be surprising.

Chapter 4
Race for the H-bomb

Standing on the steps of 10 Downing Street on the afternoon of 23 September 1949, British Prime Minister Clement Attlee read a brief statement: 'His Majesty's Government has evidence that within recent weeks an atomic explosion has occurred in the USSR.' Apart from a call for greater effort towards international control of atomic weapons, the statement offered no further explanation. The announcement did not say when and where the explosion had taken place or how it had been detected, although it later came to light that the announcement came nearly a full month after the actual explosion – the test, of a plutonium type, had been conducted on 29 August – and had been detected after the fact by spy aircraft taking air samples. None of that was revealed at the time, though. Journalists frantically trying to flesh out the story found other government officials equally tight-lipped. The public reception of the news was remarkably subdued. When the BBC led off its evening news broadcast with that news, the report was typically matter-of-fact. Across the Atlantic, President Harry Truman issued a similar statement more or less simultaneously. It, too, offered few details but tried to pre-empt a domestic political outcry with reassurances that the inevitability that the Soviets would someday develop the bomb 'has always been taken into account by us'. The implications were uncertain but the message was clear. The American atomic monopoly was over sooner than most serious observers expected. For the British people, it was a reminder that their small, densely populated islands were highly vulnerable to the new weapons. For the American people, protected by time and space, the sense of imminent peril was always going to be less immediate.

Public surprise that the Soviets had perfected the bomb was remarkably muted. The development had come before nearly everyone expected it, but the capability was not in and of itself a cause of shock. Western forecasts for when the Soviets would cross the atomic threshold had varied widely, reflecting the dearth of hard evidence on the Soviet atomic programme. The first CIA estimate on the issue, dated 31 October 1946, predicted that the Soviets would produce a bomb 'at some time between 1950 and 1953'. Later estimates put greater emphasis on the latter end of that time span. Just five days before the Soviets exploded their first bomb, the CIA predicted that the 'earliest possible date' that the Soviets would be able to develop the bomb was mid-1950, but the 'most probable date' was mid-1953. Several policymakers contributed their own guesses. The American ambassador in Moscow, Walter Bedell Smith, who later became director of central intelligence, told James Forrestal at the height of the Berlin blockade in September 1948 that it would be at least five years before the Soviets developed the bomb. 'They may well have the "notebook" know-how,' he told Forrestal, 'but not the industrial complex to translate that abstract knowledge into concrete weapons.' Sir Henry Tizard, head of the British Atomic Energy Programme, placed the date at 1957 or 1958. Some argued that it would be later. Others argued that the Soviets would never surmount the technological difficulties of the process. Even the worst-case scenarios envisaged by groups within the US air force projected that it would be 1952 or 1953.

The announcement was covered extensively in the world press, but generally the popular reaction was relatively calm. Some even used the absence of detailed information to question whether the Soviet explosion had really taken place. The public announcements of the bomb had refused to give any information on how the blast had been detected, which in turn fuelled claims from radical isolationists in Congress, such as Senator Owen Brewster (R-Maine), that the Soviet Union did not, in fact, have an atomic bomb. Doubters were aided by the absence of a follow-up performance by the Soviets. Not until two years later did the Soviets test their second atomic device. On 24 September 1951, the Air Force Atomic Energy Detection System picked up unusually intense acoustic signals within the Soviet Union, which were later confirmed to be another atomic explosion.

Re-evaluations of Soviet atomic capabilities in light of the news were that the Soviet stockpile would rise from about two a month to a total of about five or more a month by the end of 1950. That would reap, according to US intelligence estimates, a growth from approximately a 10–20 atomic bomb stockpile that the Soviets were likely to have by mid-1950 to about 200 by mid-1954. That figure constituted something of a critical threshold in American military planning. American defence planners had decided that once the Soviets had the capability to deliver approximately 200 atomic bombs to targets in the United States, they would be able to take out many of the most critical American targets and thereby inflict devastating blows to US war-fighting ability.

America's atomic monopoly

The United States moved surprisingly slowly in these early days to articulate a coherent strategic policy linking military planning to foreign policy objectives. For just over four years the United States had enjoyed an atomic monopoly. During that time, Washington, along with their closest transatlantic allies, especially Great Britain, had failed to craft a coherent doctrine that brought the awesome power of atomic weapons into the service of Western foreign policy, even as the consensus grew that the West was in a new kind of war with the Communist regime in the Soviet

Union. All they could muster were relatively hollow threats on an ad hoc basis. It was an approach US Secretary of Defense James Forrestal complained was 'a patchwork job'. Having formally adopted the concept of the 'containment' of Soviet Communism in late November 1948, most policymakers within the Truman administration simply assumed, or perhaps hoped is a better word, that the American atomic monopoly would somehow intimidate the Soviets from breaches of the peace for fear of precipitating an all-out war.

But if that was Truman's intention, it did not appear to work. The bomb was supposed to be the 'winning weapon', but by 1948 it was abundantly clear that the West was neither winning the Cold War nor preventing Moscow from repeatedly challenging Western interests. The Soviets seemed to have the initiative on all the fronts that mattered. French strategist Raymond Aron wrote in 1954 that 'When one surveys the entire period since the Hiroshima explosion, it is difficult to resist the impression that the United States has lost rather than gained by its famous atomic monopoly. It has been of no use in the Cold War.' The political crises just seemed to keep coming: Yugoslavia, Iran, Greece, Italy, France, and Germany. And underpinning the entire debate on whether the bomb would be used was the issue of whether or not it *could* be used.

Attention now turned to building a real atomic capability. Political pressure to bring the boys back home and create a smooth economic transition from war footing to peace led to a massive demobilization in the wake of World War II. There were higher domestic priorities than gearing up for another war. In the perennial guns-or-butter debate, guns lost out. For those most concerned about the emerging threat of the Soviet Union, such as James Forrestal, the demobilization went too far. Anxiety was becoming prevalent amongst American military planners that the post-war demobilization had left the United States military barely able to maintain its existing commitments; if the Soviets forced military action in another theatre, there were simply not enough Western forces to stop them. The limits were political, not economic or logistical. In contrast with the other great powers, the United States had emerged from World War II on a solid economic footing; its territory was unharmed and its fabric of society intact. All it took to reverse the weakening of American defence forces, critics of the Truman administration's low defence spending limits argued, was the political will to do so.

A by-product of the post-war demobilization was that the US atomic programme had nearly ground to a halt. In his announcement of the bombing of Hiroshima, Truman implied that atomic bombs were rolling off the assembly line: 'In their present form these bombs are now in production and even more powerful forms are in development.' While not technically incorrect, it was deliberately misleading. In fact, the Americans had only a handful of bombs then and through the early Cold War, the result of political decisions taken in Washington rather than any logistical limits. By the end of 1945, the United States had built only six atomic bombs; by 1947, only 32; by 1948, 110. By the end of 1949, when the Soviets detonated their first atomic bomb, the United States had 235 weapons. The stockpile grew at much faster rates after 1950, when Truman authorized a massive military build-up on the back of the Korean War.

Building more bombs would accomplish little without devising a viable nuclear doctrine and declaratory policy. The first Cold War crisis to test these elements was the crisis in Berlin in 1948, the first of the Cold War's genuine nuclear crises. One observer claims that in view of the precedent it was setting, 'it is clear beyond any shadow of doubt that this was the most critical crisis of the Cold War'. When Stalin blockaded Berlin in mid-1948, it seemed to provide the tangible proof that was hitherto lacking from the warnings of Forrestal and others that not only did the Soviets have a conflict of interests with the United States, but they were also willing to act upon those interests. In response, Truman made a remarkable commitment to maintain the presence in Berlin, although he had little idea how he would accomplish this. The most famous response to the challenge was the Berlin airlift, an ingenious effort to supply the 2 million residents of the Western sectors of the city by air. But Truman never regarded the airlift as anything more than a delaying tactic.

The Joint Chiefs of Staff had made it abundantly clear that there was no way to win a conventional war in Europe against the Red Army. Although some top-secret American war plans tried to incorporate the use of atomic bombs, it remained unclear how the new weapons could best contribute to the effort. Military planners hoped that the atomic bomb would be a 'distinct advantage' in war with the Soviet Union, at the same time as recognizing that the geography and structure of the Soviet Union offered relatively few high-value targets. Targeting cities such as Moscow and Leningrad was logistically viable but offered many disadvantages with little gain – against a country that had lost in the order of 27 million lives in World War II, the shock value was likely to be muted and the move was unlikely to contribute to victory. World War II had shown the value in attacking the enemy's war-making potential with strategic air power, but the Soviet Union was very different from Japan or Germany. The Soviet transportation system, identified by planners as 'the most vital cog in the war machine of the USSR', spanned vast distances with relatively few dense hubs; it was simply too spread out to be a viable target for the relatively few atomic bombs the United States possessed during the period. Soviet military industries were also dispersed, and only the country's petroleum supplies appeared vulnerable to strategic bombing. Not until 1956 did the National Security Council believe that the United States had the capability to carry out a 'decisive strike' against the Soviet Union.

The post-war demobilization had seriously depleted the practicable options available to the president to exploit the atomic monopoly, and it was further hampered by the extreme secrecy surrounding information related to atomic weapons. Not even the president was able to get a straight answer on how many weapons were in the US stockpile and what they could do. Catalysed by the apparent military impotence revealed by the absence of any good options to deal with the Berlin blockade, the Joint Chiefs of Staff undertook to review the defence posture of the United States, beginning with nuclear strategy. Forrestal and the Joint Chiefs of Staff used the blockade in their efforts to thwart Truman's tight defence budgets, seizing the opportunity to argue that relying on a perception of strength was not enough; it had to be backed up by tangible military capabilities. At the height of the Berlin blockade, frustrated by Truman's reluctance to commit to 'whether or not we are to use the A-bomb in war', Forrestal took it upon himself to authorize the Joint Chiefs to base their war planning on the assumption that nuclear weapons *would* be used.

Furthermore, the blockade demonstrated the inadequacy of American nuclear strategy when Washington was forced to improvise an atomic deterrent by sending B-29 'atomic' bombers to Britain and Germany. It was a bluff.

Few had thought seriously about how to wage atomic war. Winston Churchill suggested presenting the Soviets with an ultimatum threatening that if they did not retire from Berlin, abandon East Germany, and retreat to the Polish border, US atomic bombers would raze Soviet cities. The US Commander in Germany, General Lucius D. Clay, took a similar line by telling Forrestal that he 'would not hesitate to use the atomic bomb and would hit Moscow and Leningrad first'. British Foreign Minister Ernest Bevin was also enthusiastic for the opportunity to show Moscow 'we mean business'.

As tempting as it was to lash out at Moscow, Washington was inclined to tread lightly. As official British government policy put it, it seemed doubtful that the West could add the 'scorpion's sting' to such nuclear threats, a point that US policymakers quietly conceded. That Stalin had provocatively blockaded Berlin in the first place, despite the American atomic monopoly, was clear evidence that a deterrent had to be manufactured and explicit; the mere existence of atomic weapons was not enough. Moreover, the United States, many feared, had made commitments that exceeded its military capabilities.

The Soviet bomb

Stalin publicly professed indifference to the deterrent effect of the bomb. It was a premonition of the wide gap between Soviet and American understanding of nuclear deterrence that became entrenched in following decades 'The atomic bomb', he claimed in remarks published in *Pravda* in September 1946, 'is intended to frighten people with weak nerves, but it cannot decide the fate of a war'. Instead, he maintained an unshakeable faith that so-called permanent operating factors would ensure that the Soviet Union prevailed in any future war as they had in the last.

Stalin's calculated indifference was a strategic gambit. It was useful politically and diplomatically, but intentionally masked reality. Behind this public façade, Stalin's private comments and directions showed a more nuanced understanding of the potential impact of the atomic bomb on international relations. His own scientists had alerted him by May 1942 that the British and Americans might be jointly seeking an atomic bomb – in fact, he knew about the Manhattan Project even before Harry Truman did – but he was slow to grasp the import of the new weapon. He had been sceptical at first that such a weapon was significant; when his intelligence directorate informed him that some reports indicated that the British and Americans were collaborating on an atomic bomb, he voiced suspicions that it was part of a deliberate misinformation programme. Once convinced – paradoxically, by the suspicious absence of scientific information appearing in journals from Anglo-American government efforts to keep information from the Germans rather than any positive confirmation – Stalin clearly grasped the significance of the bomb. Pavel Sudoplatov, a former Soviet spy, claims that when a senior Soviet scientist suggested in October 1942 simply asking Churchill and Roosevelt about the programme, Stalin responded that 'You are politically naïve if you think that they would share information about the weapons that will dominate the world in the future', a comment as interesting for its evident suspicion of his allies as for his recognition of the revolutionary potential of the atomic bomb.

The Soviets had started a bomb programme in 1943 through fear that the Germans might get to the bomb first, but the resources devoted to it fluctuated at a time when there were so many other pressing issues. It was, after all, a massive and expensive risk – only the United States had the luxury of territorial security, natural resources, and two billion dollars to spend on the programme. Only after Hiroshima did atomic weapons become a top priority.

Prior to then, Stalin seems to have grossly underestimated the scale of destruction wrought by the new weapon, though that doubtless changed with the dramatic evidence of the atomic bombings of Japan. But if there were any doubt that Stalin came to appreciate the potential of the bomb to alter international politics, it is clear from his orders to Soviet security chief Lavrenti Beria and the Soviet Union's leading atomic scientist Igor Kurchatov to spare no resources in ramping up the Soviet bomb programme 'on a Russian scale'. Stalin promised that the atomic scientists would be given unprecedented freedom in their work and all the material support the state could muster. 'Hiroshima has shaken the whole world. The balance has been broken', he told his scientists. 'Build the Bomb – it will remove the great danger from us.' It was a decision that had far-reaching effects on the development of a modern Soviet military-industrial complex, effectively laying the groundwork for his successors to a massive

5. Julius and Ethel Rosenberg leaving New York City Federal Court after arraignment. The couple were later convicted of espionage and executed

nuclear programme that would establish practical strategic parity with the West within two decades.

Soviet spies played an important role. While the Manhattan Project devoted most of its early security resources to protecting against German espionage, the Soviets benefited from a steady stream of detailed information – including specific blueprints – spirited out of the programme by fellow travellers and agents such as Klaus Fuchs, David Greenglass, and Julius and Ethel Rosenberg (the latter two were executed for treason in 1953).

The opening of Soviet archives in the early 1990s, together with the declassification of the so-called VENONA transcripts – translations of some 3,000 messages sent between Moscow and Soviet intelligence stations in the US in the 1940s – paint a picture of a golden age of Soviet espionage. This information, in turn, was channelled directly to the Soviet scientists by Beria's organization. At the time, the beginning of the Cold War, few in the West doubted that this intelligence directly accelerated the Soviet bomb programme.

During the Stalin years, Soviet military doctrine basically ignored nuclear weapons as offensive weapons. But there were active efforts to defend against American long-range bombers that might be armed with atomic bombs. Around 1948, anti-aircraft defences were assigned a higher priority, around the same time that Soviet scientists and the Ministry of Defence first began looking into the technology of both intercontinental ballistic missiles and anti-ballistic missiles.

Stalin's views of the atomic bomb gradually changed. Combined with the tight secrecy imposed by the Soviet regime, efforts to determine whether the Soviet leader was deterred by the American bomb are complicated. A leading scholar of Soviet foreign policy, Vladislav Zubok, has argued that Stalin's thinking on nuclear matters, like that of most leaders in the nuclear club, evolved over time. Zubok speculated that:

> If somebody had asked Stalin after Hiroshima in 1945 and again at the end of his life in late 1952, whether he believed the bomb would affect the likelihood of war in the future, he might have given two

different answers. In 1945, he would probably have said that the US atomic monopoly encouraged America's drive for world hegemony and made the prospects of war more likely. In early 1950, after the first Soviet test, he was ready to say that the correlation of forces shifted again in favor of the forces of socialism and peace.

Winston Churchill insisted that America's atomic bomb was all that held Communist advance at bay. 'Nothing stands between Europe today and complete subjugation to Communist tyranny but the atom bomb the Americans possess', he told an audience in Wales in 1948. It was a refrain he repeated often.

'Years of opportunity', or not

In retrospect, it is surprising that the world's sole atomic power, the United States, did not make more aggressive moves to prevent others from developing the bomb. That is not to say that the idea of preventive war was not debated. It had long been discussed in classified circles. Some argued that the United States had squandered its advantage, that America's greatest military asset had been wasted, a decision that could have catastrophic consequences. James Forrestal wrote in late 1947 that the remaining years of the monopoly, however long that would be, would be the West's 'years of opportunity'. As early as January 1946, General Leslie Groves, the military commander of the Manhattan Project, reflected: 'If we were ruthlessly realistic, we would not permit any foreign power with which we are not firmly allied ... to make or possess atomic weapons. If such a country started to make atomic weapons we would destroy its capacity to make them before it had progressed far enough to threaten us.' None the less, the US government never came close to implementing a preventive war strategy and the most powerful government officials did not support the idea.

The sense of foreboding ran deep in policymaking circles about what the Soviets might do if they had the bomb, leading to a full range of prescriptions. Talk of preventive war was controversial, but held a mantle of respectability that peaked in the late 1940s and early 1950s, a respectability that faded rapidly in the midst of the thermonuclear revolution of hydrogen warheads and long-range ballistic missiles.

Although the American public remained decidedly cool to the idea of preventive war – various polls in the early 1950s pegged public support for preventive war against the Soviet Union at between 10% and 15% – support for the idea of waging war on the Soviets before Stalin built up his own large atomic arsenal enjoyed remarkably wide, if publicity-shy, support in official Washington, and Moscow knew it. Some of this was predictable.

The air force and the RAND Corporation acted as loci for the idea of preventive war and remained havens for it long after it had been discredited in other circles. But in the late 1940s and early 1950s, when there was still an apparent window of opportunity, support for preventive war also came from less expected quarters. Leading atomic scientist Leó Szilárd reportedly advocated preventive war as early as October 1945. George Kennan and fellow State Department Kremlinologist Charles Bohlen, both relative moderates in terms of Cold War military policy, found the logic compelling.

There were a number of reasons why such arguments never won the day. To begin with, it was a question of national character. America was not in the habit of starting wars. Having been on the receiving end of the surprise attack at Pearl Harbor, US policymakers – and the American public – presumably held US foreign policy to a higher standard. Although the United States had long reserved the right to take preventive military action, actually doing so would first have to overcome deeply held national convictions that starting wars was not the best way to behave in the international arena.

More important, though, were doubts that preventive war against the Soviet Union would be successful. The post-war demobilization placed severe limits on US military capabilities and the Western European allies were in no position to make any meaningful military contribution to the effort. The Red Army, which Stalin maintained in large numbers as his own form of 'deterrent', would have had a clear run to the English Channel. This in turn raised two questions: To be effective, would not preventive war have required more than air strikes with A-bombs? And would not the United States have been required to send in ground troops to occupy the Russian heartland? The plain fact was that the United States was neither capable nor inclined to wage a preventive war against the Soviet Union to prevent a communist bomb.

The thermonuclear decision

Clearly, Moscow had not been awed by the American atomic monopoly. And now that that monopoly had been broken, many observers were convinced that the Soviets would become even more dangerous. Informed opinion, including the intelligence community, recognized that it would still take time for the Soviets to develop a usable stockpile – by 1950, the Soviets had approximately 5 atomic weapons to the United States' 369. The United States faced two potential paths. One was to seize the opportunity to push for bilateral disarmament. The Soviets had baulked at early efforts at international control of atomic weapons on the basis that they would be relinquishing the right to develop their own atomic capability while the United States retained its arsenal. Now that both powers had the bomb, it would in effect be a mutual sacrifice. The other potential path was to engage in full-scale competition and an arms race. For a variety of reasons, mostly derived with the Cold War mindset, the administration chose the latter course. It was a watershed moment.

Nevertheless, hawks inside government continued to push their agenda. James Forrestal had long complained that the tight budget ceilings imposed by President Truman were forcing 'a minimum, not an adequate strategy'. His successor, Louis Johnson, was ideologically inclined towards fiscal restraint and not overly inclined towards challenging his commander-in-chief's budget directives. Given the string of Cold War setbacks – especially the Soviet atomic test, and the 'loss' of China to Mao Zedong's Communist Party, both in 1949 – political pressure eventually pushed Truman towards reconsidering defence spending and the strategy to go along with it. By the end of the process, defence spending increased by 458% by the fiscal year 1952 over the budget for the fiscal year 1951, and the level of manpower in the Defense Department was raised to nearly 5 million from a 1951 level of 2.2 million.

During the winter of 1949–50, a highly classified debate had been raging in defence and scientific circles over whether to proceed with a new generation of weapon, this one exploiting the energy released when hydrogen atoms were fused rather than split, as they were in an atomic bomb. The new kind of weapon, variously termed a hydrogen, thermonuclear, or just nuclear bomb was informally dubbed 'the super', a reference to its potential to dwarf even the explosive power of an atomic bomb. Preliminary research into such a weapon had been undertaken within the Manhattan Project by a team of scientists led by physicist Edward Teller. But with no hope of immediate success and with military budgets shrinking in the post-war economic environment, the research was halted. Based on theoretical data, Teller predicted that a hydrogen bomb would be several hundred times more powerful than the Hiroshima bomb, capable of devastating an area of hundreds of square miles, with radiation travelling much farther.

The debate centred on whether such a weapon was needed, the morality of its manufacture, and the impact its development would have on relations with Moscow. Producing a bitter mood, it eventually split not only the policymakers but also the atomic scientists themselves. In January 1950, Truman received a delegation headed by Dean Acheson, now secretary of state, which advocated development of the hydrogen bomb. After a meeting lasting only seven minutes, the president decided to press ahead with the research, despite the fact that there was no hard evidence that the hydrogen bomb would ever become a reality, and a number of scientists claimed that it couldn't be done. Many more others, including James Conant and J. Robert Oppenheimer, the physicist who had led the Los Alamos team during the Manhattan Project, argued that it was unnecessary. Even Albert Einstein came out publicly against developing the hydrogen bomb:

> The idea of achieving security through national armaments is, at the present state of military technique, a disastrous illusion ... The armament race between the USA and the USSR, originally supposed to be a preventive measure, assumes hysterical character.

The Atomic Energy Commission's own advisory committee emphasized that the hydrogen bomb lent itself to genocide but not much else:

> The use of this weapon would bring about the destruction of innumerable human lives; it is not a weapon which can be used exclusively for the destruction of material installations of military or semi-military purposes. Its use therefore carries much further than the atomic bomb itself the policy of exterminating civilian populations.

Truman's statement announcing his directive betrayed none of the drama of the top-secret debate behind the scenes. In a brief, spare statement that included the usual call for greater international control of atomic arms, Truman announced that:

> It is part of my responsibility as Commander in Chief of the Armed Forces to see to it that our country is able to defend itself against

Race for the H-bomb

55

any possible aggressor. Accordingly, I have directed the Atomic Energy Commission to continue its work on all forms of atomic weapons, including the so-called hydrogen or superbomb. Like all other work in the field of atomic weapons, it is being and will be carried forward on a basis consistent with the overall objectives of our program for peace and security.

It was a momentous decision, paving the way for the thermonuclear revolution and the arms race that went along with it.

The sense of urgency forced quick action. A few weeks after Truman's announcement, Louis Johnson, at the prompting of the Joint Chiefs of Staff, requested 'immediate implementation of all-out development of hydrogen bombs and means for their production and delivery'. By early March 1950, the thermonuclear weapon programme had been ramped up to 'a matter of the highest urgency'.

The same day that Truman authorized development of the hydrogen bomb, he instructed Acheson and Louis Johnson to reassess the Soviet threat in light of the Soviet Union's nascent atomic capability and recent Cold War developments. Under the direction of Paul H. Nitze, Kennan's successor as director of the State Department's Policy Planning Staff, a group of state and defence officials formulated a comprehensive statement of a national security strategy and submitted it to the president in early April 1950. Known by its bureaucratic designation as NSC 68 'United States Objectives and Programs for National Security', the document was deliberately alarmist and made the case for a massive build-up in resources and a hardening of strategy to go along with it. With its urgent tone and blunt, hawkish policy prescriptions, the document reflected a change in direction in policy terms, but its substance expressed the mood of many Washington policymakers that had been brewing for some time.

NSC 68 was fundamentally concerned with the problem of 'weapons of mass destruction' (the first to introduce the term to policy documents). It estimated that 'within the next four years, the USSR will attain the capability of seriously damaging vital centers of the United States, provided it strikes a first blow and provided further that the blow is opposed by no more effective opposition than we now have programmed'. It warned that once the Soviet Union 'has a sufficient atomic capability to make a surprise attack on us, nullifying our atomic superiority and creating a military situation decisively in its favor, the Kremlin might be tempted to strike swiftly and with stealth'. In these circumstances, and estimating the prospects of the international control of atomic energy as negligible, Nitze and his associates suggested that the United States had little choice but to increase its atomic and, if possible, its thermonuclear capabilities as rapidly as it could. The atomic stockpile should be rapidly increased and the hydrogen bomb programme continued at a greatly accelerated pace.

NSC 68 also warned of the dangers of 'piecemeal aggression' whereby the Soviets could threaten American interests without resorting to direct military confrontation. By exploiting Washington's unwillingness to use its atomic weapons unless directly attacked, Moscow might pose a military threat by other, more abstruse methods, which could potentially throw American defence policy into disarray and bypass whatever limited effect the atomic deterrent might be having. When North Korean troops marched on South Korea on 25 June 1950, at the height of the internal administration debate over NSC 68, it posed what was in many ways a novel challenge; it was not a scenario anticipated by existing Western strategy. In the words of one leading French strategist, Raymond Aron, 'The Korean War had taught world leaders that there are more things in heaven and earth than in models.' The Soviet preponderance of conventional military forces, compounded by an incipient atomic capability, which included a 'probable fission capability and possible thermonuclear capability', posed a serious challenge for which military planners strove to account. Consequently, it provoked a comprehensive reappraisal of US national security assumptions and seemed to lend weight to arguments for embracing NSC 68.

Beyond the realm of logic

The decision had at once profound effects on nuclear weapons development and nuclear policy. The atomic arsenal received new emphasis, with American science and technology engaged in producing smaller and cheaper atomic warheads that permitted the US army to deploy thousands of tactical atomic weapons on the battlefield. Nuclear research and development was boosted by the desire of each branch of the armed services for a piece of the action. During the 1950s, the army turned its attention to intermediate-range, land-based, ballistic missiles, and the navy, first, to aircraft-carrier-based atomic bombers and then to nuclear-powered and armed submarines. But the mainstays of US strategic forces continued to be the bombers of the Strategic Air Command. More importantly, work was accelerated on the H-bomb project, and on 31 October 1952, the United States detonated its first thermonuclear device, in the Pacific.

The explosion was the culmination of an extraordinary effort on the part of the Truman administration to maintain its ascendancy over the Soviet Union on the nuclear ladder and provided a watershed for deterrence. With the opening phases of the thermonuclear revolution now a reality, policymakers struggled to comprehend the scale of destruction of the new technology. Edward Teller had predicted in 1947 that the new weapon would be capable of devastating an area of 300 or 400 square miles and that radiation could well travel much farther. In terms of military strategy, such a regional scale clearly changed the whole nature of the weapon. But it didn't take long to grasp that such a weapon might well transform the nature of war and peace themselves. As Churchill put it, 'The atomic bomb, with all its terror, did not carry us outside the scope of human control or manageable events in thought or action, in peace or war. But ... [with] the hydrogen bomb, the entire foundation of human affairs was revolutionized.'

While recognition of this exacerbated psychological gap between strategic weapons and victory prompted a sharpened focus of strategic thought that lasted at least for a decade and a half, US policymakers were forced to deal with its consequences on a more immediate level. Seasoned war leader Eisenhower declared that with the existence of employable thermonuclear weapons, 'War no longer has any logic whatever.' And to prove the point, the Soviet Union successfully detonated its first thermonuclear device less than a year later, on 12 August 1953; it was a limited explosion about 25 times smaller than the US effort. In November 1955, the Soviet successfully air-dropped an H-bomb, with an explosive power of 1.6 megatons.

Great Britain joined the atomic club on 3 October 1952, with a successful test near the Monte Bello Islands, off the coast of Australia, and the thermonuclear club on 15 May 1957, with an H-bomb explosion of 200–300 kilotons, at Christmas Islands in the Pacific. Under the relentless guidance of Charles de Gaulle, France acquired its own nuclear strike force with a test in the Sahara Desert in Algeria in 1960, followed by a thermonuclear explosion at Fanagataufa Atoll, South Pacific, in 1968. Fearful of both superpowers and with an eye on India, China joined the nuclear club in 1964 and thermonuclear club in 1967, with a bomb that was dropped over the Lop Nor test site.

During the late 1960s, Israel, under the initial direction of the 'father' of the French atom bomb, Francis Perrin, who built the Dimona Nuclear Research facility, became the sixth nation with nuclear weapons capability, though the Israeli government denies it. India (1974) and Pakistan (1998) became the seventh and eight nations to acquire nuclear status, focusing attention on their great rivalry in South Asia. And North Korea joined the nuclear club in October 2006 (see Chapter 7).

During the 1970s, South Africa's Atomic Energy Board established a nuclear weapons programme. Using largely open sources, they enriched uranium. In August 1977, a Soviet satellite discovered South Africa's nuclear test site in the Kalahari Desert; however, under pressure from the United States, the USSR, and France, South Africa temporarily postponed its plans until 1982, by which time it had developed its first complete nuclear device. Then, for reasons very much of its own, one suspects, South Africa closed down its nuclear weapons programme and dismantled its weapons facilities in 1989. Two years later, it joined the Nuclear Non-Proliferation Treaty (see Chapter 7).

While opposition to nuclear energy first emerged shortly after the atomic bomb was built, significant anti-nuclear opposition did not emerge until the 1950s. The American hydrogen bomb test on the Bikini Atoll in March 1954 made the world acutely conscious of radioactive fallout for the first time. Fallout from the explosion rained down on the Marshall Islanders and a Japanese fishing boat, the hapless *Lucky Dragon*. Shortly afterwards, a handful of London housewives started a campaign to pressure the US government to stop its nuclear testing, and this became the beginning of the test ban movement which provided the drumbeat and groundwork for the Comprehensive Nuclear Test Ban Treaty four decades later. The initial protest later became the National Campaign for Nuclear Disarmament, of which British philosopher-mathematician Bertrand Russell was the guiding spirit. If war no longer had any logic, nor did the further testing of nuclear weapons.

Chapter 5
Nuclear deterrence and arms control

When, at the end of the 1970s, Queen Elizabeth declared that nuclear weaponry's 'awesome destructive power has preserved the world from a major war for the past thirty-five years', she reflected an opinion held by most Cold War statesmen and, subsequently, by many academics. Later, historian John Lewis Gaddis viewed the 45-year Cold War as 'the long peace' since there were no direct major hostilities between the United States and the Soviet Union. It was an unprecedented accomplishment, he argued, as 'prior to that moment, improvements in weaponry had, with very few exceptions, increased the costs of fighting wars without reducing the propensity to do so'. In this sense, then, the nuclear revolution was akin to a great earthquake, setting off a series of shockwaves that gradually worked their way through the political system.

But not all observers agreed. Some suggested that nuclear weapons were 'essentially irrelevant' to keeping the peace because, even without these new destructive devices, a world war had become too costly for a rational leadership to engage in it. A former State Department official, Raymond L. Garthoff, acknowledged the existence of nuclear weaponry in the hands of both superpowers undoubtedly exercised 'a restraining, deterring, effect'. But had nuclear weapons not existed, he concluded, 'it remains highly probable that neither the United States nor the Soviet Union would have attacked the other, and less certain but also probable that neither would have taken other military actions so provocative as to have precipitated general war between the two powers'.

There is little likelihood of agreement on the general proposition that the destructive power of nuclear weapons maintained a relative peace between the superpowers. But an important caveat should be inserted. In 1985, for example, Lord Carrington, the Secretary General of NATO, stated his belief in the value of deterrence: 'I don't believe it's worked; I *know* it's worked. There hasn't been a war for 40 years.... there is [no] other way at the present time of keeping the peace for the world.' In referring to 'keeping the peace for the world', he was speaking of the absence of a nuclear war, since non-nuclear powers continued to wage conventional war freely, though nuclear powers less freely.

Wars fought with conventional weaponry were a common occurrence during the Cold War and could be waged by non-nuclear powers with little restraint. Nuclear powers could wage a limited conventional war, but they were restrained from fighting one another. Case studies of Cold War-era conflicts suggest two ironclad, unwritten rules: first, no nuclear power may use military force against another nuclear power; and, second, a nuclear power, using military force against a non-nuclear nation, may not use nuclear weapons. Moreover, possessing nuclear weapons did not necessarily deter a non-nuclear nation from waging war with a client state of a nuclear power, as the United States found out in the Korean and Vietnam Wars.

Evolution of nuclear deterrence

Not until the second decade of the nuclear age was the danger of nuclear weaponry and the perception of this danger sufficient to give rise to the concept of deterrence and create a Cold

War stalemate. Eugene Rabinowitch, editor of the *Bulletin of the Atomic Scientists*, chose 1956 as the birth date of the 'Age of Deterrence', calling it AD I, 'the first year of deterrence'. Subsequently, others dated its arrival from 1954, 1955, or 1957. The *Random House Dictionary* (1987) chose 1955 as the date of its appearance, and defined it as 'The distribution of nuclear weapons among nations such that no nation will initiate an attack

---

Stages of weapons development

Research and Development (R&D): This period can take from a year or two to more than 10 years, during which concepts and basic technologies are explored.

Engineering and Manufacturing Development (EMD): It can take five years or more to engineer and develop the industrial processes to manufacture and assemble a system.

Developmental Testing: This is conducted throughout the R&D and EMD phases to learn about the strengths and weaknesses of the new system and to apply these technologies in a military environment.

Operational Testing: This is conducted with production equipment in realistic operational environments – at night, in bad weather, against realistic countermeasures.

Production: Initial quantities are usually small and later, after successful operational testing, a system may go into 'full-rate production'.

Deployment: The fielding of the new system, either in large or small quantities, in military units to develop or enhance tactics, techniques, and procedures for the use of the system if that has not already been done in the development phase.

Philip E. Coyle,
Arms Control Today 32: 4 (May 2002): 5

for fear of retaliation.' The standoff was also known as the 'balance of terror', a phrase made famous by Winston Churchill, but this was a bit too stark for popular consumption, while the term 'deterrence' was more easily digested.

With the advent of thermonuclear devices (H-bombs) and the introduction of nuclear-tipped, long-range ballistic missiles by the late 1950s, the concept of nuclear deterrence gained widespread currency. As the nuclear arsenals expanded in the 1960s, the phrases 'deterrence policy' and 'deterrence strategy' were used as euphemisms for 'nuclear policy' (short for 'nuclear weapons policy') and 'nuclear strategy'. And strategic theorists gradually linked words such as 'credible', 'effective', 'stable', and 'mutual' to the concept of a nuclear balance or deterrence.

These theorists also speculated about possible methods of employing the expanding nuclear arsenals. A 'first strike' could take place when a nation thought it had sufficient nuclear forces to overwhelm its foe and thus achieve victory, while a closely related 'pre-emptive strike' would call for launching a nuclear strike when a nation anticipated its enemy was preparing a first strike. A 'retaliatory strike' or 'second strike' capability referred to a nation's ability to absorb a nuclear first strike and still retain sufficient weapons to inflict unacceptable damage on its attacker or at least what is hoped would be unacceptable.

Policymakers and the public, however, rarely saw strategies in such stark forms. Thus deterrence emerged as neither a military strategy nor policy; it was simply recognized as a political reality. When the US and USSR governments believed their military services were able to absorb a nuclear first strike and still possess sufficient forces for retaliatory strikes – as they did by the end of the 1960s – mutual deterrence had arrived, in fact, if not in formal policy.

If deterrence gradually became mutual, the perceptions and policies of the two superpowers had diverged at the very onset of the Cold War. Their socio-political systems, grounded on differing ideological, geopolitical, economic, and political ambitions, created serious concerns about the designs and intentions of each other. 'For more than four decades,' Strobe Talbott lamented in *Time* magazine, 'Western policy has been based on a grotesque exaggeration of what the USSR could do if it wanted, therefore what it might do, therefore what the West must be prepared to do in response.' This led to grossly exaggerated worst-case assumptions about Soviet capabilities. At the same time, a disturbing change had begun to take place in the United States as militarism insinuated itself into American life. The scepticism about arms and armies that informed American society from its founding had started to vanish. Political leaders, liberals and conservatives alike, became enamoured of military might. The Soviet ambassador to Washington, Anatoly Dobrynin, acknowledged in his memoirs that Moscow's Cold War policies were also unreasonably dominated by ideology, and this produced continued confrontation. The superpowers, Mikhail Gorbachev later concluded, had been mesmerized by ideological myths.

These ideological and political tensions resulted in the adoption of different strategies to avoid a nuclear showdown. As a consequence, the United States addressed the problem of preventing war almost exclusively in terms of military capabilities. The Soviet Union, for its part, addressed preventing war primarily in terms of political motivations and intentions. The different focus of the two powers had important effects on the military doctrines and forces of each.

Throughout the Cold War, American leaders usually pursued a nuclear strategy that was, in the end, contradictory. For example, President Harry Truman was convinced that, on the one hand, nuclear weapons played an essential role in the democratic world's defence against its enemies, but, on the other hand, he feared that a war involving nuclear weapons most likely would destroy the US and modern civilization. In his January 1953 farewell address, Truman declared 'starting an atomic war is totally unthinkable for rational men'. This was, he later stated, 'because it affects the civilian population and murders them by wholesale'. President Dwight Eisenhower would come to view war with thermonuclear weapons as 'preposterous'. Yet as these and subsequent administrations acknowledged that nuclear war was 'unthinkable', American political leaders and military chiefs continued to seek nuclear arsenals that might advance their more limited political objectives.

The Truman administration sought to tie the idea of deterrence to a way of enforcing the new policy of containment that was intended to prevent – and eventually reverse – the indirect and direct expansion of Soviet domination and influence. The administration's basic national strategy of containment sought not only to 'block further expansion of Soviet power', but 'by all means short of war' to 'induce a retraction of the Kremlin's control and influence ... to check and to roll back the Kremlin's drive for world domination'. Washington hoped its atomic monopoly might expand the theory of deterrence (preventing a nuclear attack on the US) to include the possibility of 'compellence' (forcing a Soviet withdrawal from Eastern Europe).

The destruction of Hiroshima had little deterrent effect on Moscow, but it did prompt Soviet Premier Joseph Stalin to insist upon Russia's possession of nuclear weaponry to maintain the balance of power. And, he looked differently on the Soviet expansion into Eastern Europe – Stalin saw it as creating a barrier against any future German ambitions as well as the restoration of Russia's historic borders.

During the early Cold War years, there were a few US efforts to apply 'atomic compellence', that is, seeking to redress a situation.

Truman asserted in his memoirs that America's atomic monopoly had pressured Moscow's withdrawal from northern Azerbaijan in March 1946. Subsequent documents indicated the Soviets were not moved by the threats.

In secret discussions during crises of 1953–5, President Dwight Eisenhower insisted that the use of atomic weapons 'was neither unthinkable nor unwinnable'. When he implied a willingness to employ conventional and nuclear force to resolve issues arising from the Korean armistice, Indo-China, and the Nationalist Chinese offshore islands, Eisenhower was persuaded that Moscow would not intervene to aid China or escalate a local conflict that risked a confrontation with the US's superior nuclear forces. In an effort to get 'more bang for the buck', Eisenhower launched his 'New Look' programme that trimmed funds for the army and navy, while increasing monies allotted to expand the strategic air command (SAC) and increase America's nuclear arsenal.

Secretary of State John Foster Dulles' infamous 1954 essay in *Time* magazine, 'A Policy of Boldness', further embellished the administration's effort at 'atomic compellance'. Regional allies must be supported by 'massive retaliatory power', he argued. 'The way to deter aggression is for the free community to be willing and able to respond vigorously at places and with means of its own choosing.' It is uncertain that any of these threats altered Soviet or Chinese decision policies; but it certainly upset many in the foreign policy public who pointed out that the major Communist regimes had limited influence in many local conflicts such as the Indo-China conflict.

Subsequently, three developments alarmed the American public and challenged Eisenhower's defence policies. On 22 November 1955, the Soviets surprised the administration by detonating an H-bomb; in August 1957, they tested an intercontinental ballistic missile; and in October, the Soviets startled the world by launching Sputnik I, the first orbiting artificial satellite. Public unease persuaded the president to create a commission, led by Rowan Gaither, to assess the nation's vulnerability. The Gaither report, titled 'Deterrence and Survival in the Nuclear Age', released on 7 November 1957, held that the Soviets would have a dozen operational intercontinental ballistic missiles within a year, while it would take the US two or three years to catch up – creating a 'missile gap'. (President John F. Kennedy quickly learned it was the Soviets who faced a 'missile gap'.)

In July 1958, Eisenhower was presented with two alarming scenarios: in the first, a Soviet nuclear strike that 'wiped out' the federal government and destroyed the nation's economy; in the second, the Soviets destroyed all SAC bases and still wreaked havoc on the nation. In the US's retaliation the Soviets would suffer approximately three times the US damage, but American losses were staggering at nearly 65% of a population of nearly 178 million souls. Stunned, Eisenhower's views changed dramatically – in a general war, he concluded, there could be no winners – thus thermonuclear weaponry could only be used to deter.

Mutual assured destruction (MAD)

The policy of massive retaliation was formally replaced in September 1967 by Secretary of Defense Robert McNamara's recognition that the Soviet nuclear build-up was approaching parity, thus creating a situation of 'assured destruction' (critic Donald Brennen added 'mutual' to get the acronym of MAD). The idea of MAD did not sit well with American military chiefs preaching peace through strength. The 'first principle of deterrence', General Thomas S. Powers wrote in 1965, was 'to maintain a credible capability to achieve a military victory under any set of conditions or circumstances'. An angry air force General Curtis LeMay insisted, 'The deterrent philosophy we now pursue has drained away our red military blood.'

Nonetheless, with their budgets at stake, the US military devised a formula (the triad) that provided each service with a strategic function. The air force possessed strategic bombers and nuclear-tipped intercontinental ballistic missiles (ICBMs), the navy its submarine-launched ballistic missiles (SSBMs), and the army its intermediate-range ballistic missiles (IRBMs), nuclear artillery, and mines, as well as anti-missile defences. In theory, at least, the nuclear triad reduced the chances that an enemy could destroy all of a country's nuclear forces in a first-strike attack, ensuring that a devastating second-strike response could be carried out.

Ballistic missile basics

Ballistic missiles are classified by the maximum distance that they can travel, which is a function of the missile's engines and the weight of the missile's warhead. To add more distance to a missile's range, rockets are stacked on top of each other in a configuration referred to as staging.

There are four general classifications of ballistic missiles:

- *Short-range ballistic missiles*, travelling less than 1,000 kilometres (approximately 620 miles).

- *Medium-range ballistic missiles*, travelling between 1,000–3,000 kilometres (approximately 620–1,860 miles).

- *Intermediate-range ballistic missiles*, travelling between 3,000–5,500 kilometres (approximately 1,860–3,410 miles).

- *Intercontinental ballistic missiles* (ICBMs), travelling more than 5,500 kilometres.

Short- and medium-range ballistic missiles are referred to as theatre ballistic missiles, ICBMs are described as strategic ballistic missiles.

All ballistic missiles have three stages of flight:[1]

- *The boost phase* begins at launch and lasts until the rocket engines stop firing and pushing the missile away from Earth. Depending on the missile, this stage lasts between three and five minutes. During much of this time, the missile is travelling relatively slowly, although towards the end of this stage an ICBM can reach speeds of more than 24,000 kilometres per hour. The missile stays in one piece during this stage.

- *The midcourse phase* begins after the rockets finish firing and the missile is on a ballistic course toward its target. This is the longest stage of a missile's flight, lasting up to 20 minutes for ICBMs. During the early part of the midcourse stage, the missile is still ascending toward its apogee, while during the latter part it is descending toward Earth. It is during this stage that the missile's warhead(s), as well as any decoys, separate from the delivery vehicle.

- *The terminal phase* begins when the missile's warhead re-enters the Earth's atmosphere, and it continues until impact or detonation. This stage takes less than a minute for a strategic warhead, which can be travelling at speeds greater than 3,200 kilometres per hour.

Arms Control Today 31–34 (July/August 2002)

1 Short- and medium-range ballistic missiles may not exit the atmosphere or have a warhead that separates from its booster.

Despising notions of parity and sufficiency, defence analysts and military chiefs sought to find a way to employ nuclear weapons and a reason to expand their arsenals. For brief exhilarating moments, they tossed about the ideas of nuclear war-fighting – limited nuclear war, 'graduated deterrence', 'essential equivalence', launch on warning, pre-emption, etc. – only to be dismissed. For example, the London *Economist* found 'graduated deterrence' had two fatal defects. First, 'the deterrent, because of being graduated to the scale of aggression, would lose some of its power to deter'. Second, if the 'deterrent' were used in a limited way, the self-restraint would not be recognized as such.

Since the Soviet military did not receive nuclear weapons until 1954 and did not have sufficient delivery systems for many more years, Moscow could not rely on nuclear deterrence. Thus, the Soviet approach to averting war was basically political. In contrast to the American focus on deterrence as the essence of strategy and policy, successive Soviet leaders reacted to the nuclear age by adjustments of strategy, policy, and even ideology to give the highest priority to preventing war.

In the immediate post-World War II years, Stalin did not see the Americans and British as embarking on military conquests, and he believed he could occasionally probe the West's determination without provoking a general war. But he did miscalculate in permitting the North Koreans to attack the South and in seeking to pressure the West to withdraw from Berlin. Nonetheless, during these pre-nuclear years Soviet military plans appear to have been mainly defensive.

Stalin's successors brought deterrence into their considerations: from the mid-1950s in theory, the mid-1960s in interim real capability, and the early or mid-1970s in terms of rough parity. After the Soviets exploded a hydrogen device, Prime Minister Georgii Malenkov was the first leader to warn that a nuclear war would mean the end of world civilization. Political opponents – such as Nikita Khrushchev – denounced him for repeating Eisenhower's warning, but as these critics succeeded him, they soon sounded the same message.

In the late 1950s and early 1960s, Moscow did seek to brandish its nuclear weaponry, but it was paradoxically at the time of their greatest relative weakness. From the Suez Crisis in 1956 to the Cuban Missile Crisis in October 1962, Khrushchev attempted to turn the Soviet Union's weaknesses into a deterrent and even a political compellent by an outrageous, deceptive exaggeration of its nuclear capabilities. When Khrushchev decided to deploy Soviet MRBMs, IRBMs, tactical nuclear weapons, and nuclear-capable medium-range bombers secretly in Cuba, where they would be positioned to strike most of the continental United States within minutes, his reasoning was to bolster the Soviet deterrent. Whether he wanted to use this deterrent in an offensive or defensive role has been debated by scholars ever since. Once the deployments were discovered, John F. Kennedy responded to the challenge by implementing a naval blockade of the island and threatening military action if the missiles and bombers were not removed. After a week-long standoff, during which Strategic Air Command's forces were on airborne alert, the Soviet leader agreed to remove the missiles and a month later agreed to remove the bombers. After this spectacular failure, Moscow quit attempting to achieve political gains from a marginal nuclear arsenal. For even as the Soviets built up real nuclear forces in the 1960s and 1970s and maintained parity in the 1980s, buttressing nuclear deterrence, they never again attempted to redress the nuclear balance by force – or even the threat to use force.

What little is known of Soviet war planning (and US planning) during the Cold War points to its armed forces seeking to prevail should deterrence fail. In 1955, Marshal Pavel Rotmistrov advanced a shift in Soviet nuclear doctrine to prevent a surprise attack from crippling their retaliatory forces by endorsing a pre-emptive strike (five years after the Truman administration advanced the same concept) when an imminent enemy nuclear attack was detected. In the bomber era, he stressed, the idea of pre-emption was *not* a cover for a surprise attack or preventive war. 'The duty of the Soviet armed forces is to not permit surprise attack by the enemy on our country, and in case an attempt is made, not only to repulse the attack successfully, but also to deal to the enemy simultaneous or even pre-emptive surprise blows of terrible crushing power.' The pre-emptive doctrine was replaced in the late 1960s by launch under attack and, probably, in the 1980s by launch in retaliation.

In Washington, a debate persisted throughout the Cold War as to whether the Soviets were really prepared to accept the idea of deterrence or whether they were developing the weapons and strategy to go beyond 'defensive' deterrence. Soviet leaders, however, did not view the American concept of deterrence as either benign or defensive (as Washington did); instead they saw it as offensive – compellent and intimidating.

A question arises from this review of deterrence: how much is enough? British Laborite Denis Healey, shadow Foreign Secretary in the early 1980s, declared that only 5% of the warheads in hand were actually necessary to deter Moscow, the remaining 95% were merely to assure the general public. In its May 1992 issue, the *Bulletin of the Atomic Scientists* asked a group of specialists on nuclear topics: What is to be done with nuclear weapons? All wanted 'deep cuts' in the existing nuclear arsenals and most agreed nations should maintain 'the least amount [needed] to deter'. Many placed the desirable number of weapons to be retained at 100. Clearly, much that was done in the name of deterrence of a potential adversary was really done to provide reassurance to one's allies and one's own people.

In 1996, the Canberra Commission on the Elimination of Nuclear Weapons, an international commission of distinguished individuals that was initiated by the Australian government, reached the conclusion that 'Nuclear weapons [still] pose an intolerable threat to all humanity and its habitat, yet tens of thousands remain in arsenals built up at an extraordinary time of deep antagonism. That time has passed, yet assertions of their utility continue.' Even in 2007, when some reductions had occurred, Russia had nuclear weapons with the destructive force to destroy humanity 29 times; the United States 18 times.

That the Cold War ended with a whisper rather than mushroom clouds was at once the result of good luck and mutual prudence. In the absence of serious efforts to resolve major superpower political differences, the continued negotiations of the military-oriented arms control pacts – which included many other projects dealing with weaponry and practices than mentioned above – aided greatly in persuading Moscow and Washington, despite their often provocative rhetoric, to practise caution. But can the post-Cold War era maintain the good fortune and mutual prudence?

Arms control and nuclear stability

Arms races, according to conventional wisdom, were the result of conflicting foreign policy objectives and would, with a reduction in international political tensions, fade away. This historically grounded observation lost much relevance in the 1960s, when intercontinental ballistic missiles with nuclear-tipped warheads turned the proposition on its head. Instead of military force supporting foreign policy, managing nuclear weaponry became a major foreign policy objective. Often shrugged off as arcane and obtuse discussions, these post-1945 arms control negotiations played an important, but frequently overlooked, role. During the Cold War, arms control became the principal conduit for Soviet-American relations, and even in times of tension, arms control trudged ever on in some form or another.

Arms control and disarmament policies were advocated during the Cold War for several purposes: to enhance the nation's security, reduce military expenditures, influence international public opinion, and gain a domestic partisan political advantage. However, the overriding reason the superpowers engaged in protracted negotiations that led to many agreements was the necessity in the nuclear era of maintaining a stable international environment.

Bernard Baruch's ill-fated effort to deal with atomic weapons at the inauguration of the United Nations Atomic Energy Committee in June 1946 (discussed in Chapter 3) launched the first of what would become hundreds, if not thousands, of multilateral and bilateral discussions on arms-control measures during the next four decades. Washington's continued insistence since then upon intrusive inspection systems to verify treaty compliance, which Moscow viewed as sanctioned espionage, figured prominently in stalemating future arms-control endeavours. Some critics have argued with considerable justification that verification issues have become excessively prominent in arms-control negotiations; they also argue that the US's demands were purposely designed to impede such negotiations or, if agreed to, would greatly enhance its opportunities for general intelligence-gathering.

The arms-control activities shifted to more limited, technically oriented objectives in the 1950s, as radioactive fallout from atmospheric nuclear tests aroused worldwide efforts to halt the testing. President Eisenhower asked technical experts to develop a verification system, a move that had unexpected long-term results, since experts often complicate issues to a point where they become insoluble. After developing techniques that could distinguish between earthquakes and virtually all underground nuclear explosions, technicians kept searching to reduce the already quite low error rate. It became impossible to negotiate a comprehensive test ban because critics argued that one could not be *absolutely* certain that no cheating was going on. This overemphasis on technical details, in fact, made the problem of verifying the test ban seem more and more formidable, because the verification system demanded by the seismologically expert American politicians was always going to be too intrusive to be acceptable to the Soviet Union.

While Eisenhower obtained only an informal moratorium on testing, John F. Kennedy entered the presidency determined to negotiate a comprehensive test ban. When Ambassador W. Averell Harriman went to Moscow to finalize the test ban, in July 1963, a dividend of the resolution of the Cuban Missile Crisis, he took scientific advisers with him but deliberately excluded them from the negotiating team, emphasizing that arms-control negotiations were, fundamentally, political undertakings. As he later explained, 'The expert is to point out all the difficulties and dangers … but it is for the political leaders to decide whether the political, psychological and other advantages offset such risks as there may be.' By this time, however, it was all but certain that such a treaty was beyond reach. In addition to Senate soundings that a comprehensive treaty would not pass muster, Khrushchev had repeated his objections to its requirement of on-site inspections – the Soviet Union would never 'open its doors to NATO spies'.

Khrushchev indicated, however, that he would be willing to conclude a limited or partial test-ban treaty. Accordingly, after 10 days of tense negotiations, closely monitored and supervised by President Kennedy himself, the Treaty Banning Nuclear Weapons Tests in the Atmosphere, Outer Space, and Under Water – the Limited Test Ban Treaty – was initialled in Moscow by the principal negotiators on 25 July 1963.

When the Soviet Union achieved a crude parity in strategic weaponry in the late 1960s, American Cold Warriors called on Washington for intensified efforts to achieve US military superiority. Meanwhile, arms-control proponents, inside and outside of Washington, argued that negotiated limits on arms competition were more likely to lead to long-term security than both sides scrambling to gain a temporary military edge. 'The problem posed to both sides by this dilemma of steadily increasing military power and steadily decreasing national security', physicist and diplomat Herbert York insisted, 'has no technical solution'. Political solutions were needed.

In his 1969 inaugural address, Richard Nixon spoke of 'a new era of negotiation' in which all nations, especially the superpowers, would seek 'to reduce the burden of arms' while reinvigorating the 'structure of peace'. This could be accomplished, Nixon envisaged, through a programme of 'linkage', or détente. He and his national security adviser, Henry Kissinger, were prepared to go considerably beyond previous administrations in discussing strategic arms control and trade issues with the Soviet Union, but they expected the Kremlin to reciprocate by assisting in the resolution of ongoing disputes in Africa, the Middle East, and Southeast Asia.

In November 1969, the superpowers' delegations began bilateral talks focused on limitations of both defensive and offensive strategic weapons systems – essentially ICBMs and SLBMs. These negotiations would continue, intermittently, resulting in two strategic arms limitations treaties (SALT I and II), the intermediate-range (INF) missile pact (the only treaty that actually reduced the number of offensive nuclear weapons during the Cold War), and the strategic arms reduction talks (START I) that were finally concluded in 1991.

The SALT I pacts of May 1972 consisted of the Anti-Ballistic Missile (ABM) Treaty which limited each party to two sites, an Interim Agreement (1972–7) on strategic systems, and a political 'Basic Principles' accord. The Interim Agreement's limits on strategic systems were actually higher than each currently possessed; but it did set ceilings on future deployments. To defeat Soviet ABM systems, the US in 1967 began developing a multiple independently targeted re-entry vehicle (MIRV) which carried aloft, on a single missile, several warheads, each capable of striking a different target. Delegates might have halted

MIRV programmes during SALT I negotiations, but Pentagon and congressional opponents had warned Kissinger 'don't come back with a MIRV ban'. Three years later, when Moscow deployed its own, considerable MIRVs, the Pentagon paid for its short-sighted insistence on a temporary advantage as the MIRV deployments made a pre-emptive strike appear more promising in a crisis situation because each side's ICBMs had become vulnerable.

The 'Basic Principles of Relations' agreement was initiated by the Kremlin and, while generally ignored by the America leadership, was considered by Soviet officials as 'an important political declaration'. They hoped it would be, as Dobrynin recalled, the basis of a 'new political process of détente in our relations' because it recognized the Soviet doctrine of peaceful co-existence and acknowledged the 'principle of equality as a basis for the security of both countries'. Moscow believed the superpowers could cooperate in resolving their basic differences despite 'minor' problems in the Third World; however, Washington interpreted détente to mean that the USSR, China, and Cuba were to maintain a 'hands-off' policy in the Third World. The failure to develop détente's boundaries and to gain public acceptance doomed the idea. American hawks vigorously denounced any attempt to ameliorate relations with the Soviet Union.

President Gerald Ford and Soviet Premier Leonid Brezhnev agreed 'in principle' at Vladivostok in November 1974, that each side should be limited to 2,400 ICBMs, SLBMs, and long-range bombers, of which 1,320 could have multiple warheads; but they could not finalize a SALT II pact. After stumbling in his initial efforts, President Jimmy Carter finally agreed to a 78-page SALT II treaty in April 1979 that hewed closely to the so-called Vladivostok principles but also limited air-to-surface cruise missiles and carried an extensive list of qualitative restrictions. He failed, however, to press for its ratification.

Ronald Reagan had never, until he met Soviet leader Mikhail Gobachev, supported an arms-control treaty. He opposed the 1963 Limited Test Ban pact, the 1968 Non-Proliferation Treaty, the 1972 SALT I and ABM agreements, and denounced SALT II as 'fatally flawed'. Moreover, early in Reagan's first term, he ended negotiations for a comprehensive test ban treaty and terminated US compliance with SALT II in May 1986. Contrary to Reagan apologists, Gorbachev's concessions were essential for the arms-control accomplishments during the Reagan presidency.

In May 1982, Reagan announced a plan for a 'practical phased reduction' of strategic weaponry. If the public was enthusiastic, analysts labelled the initial START I plan non-negotiable because it required the Soviets to dismantle their best strategic weapons, while the US kept most of its Minutemen missiles, deployed one hundred of the new large MX (Missile Experimental) missiles, deployed its new cruise missiles, and modernized its submarine and bomber fleets. Attempts to modify the plan during the next four years met with interminable bickering between government agencies, prompting a senior member of the National Security Council to acknowledge 'Even if the Soviets did not exist, we might not get a START treaty because of disagreements on our side.' Another high-ranking US official complained that if the Soviets 'came to us and said, "You write it, we'll sign it," we still couldn't do it'.

As he began preparing for re-election in January 1984, President Reagan faced a multifaceted dilemma – how to ease tensions with Moscow, deflect the criticism of the anti-nuclear protestors both at home and abroad, and appease the hard-liners in the Senate eager to chastise the Soviets for alleged arms-control violations. William Casey, director of Central Intelligence, had advised Reagan that NATO's exercise ABLE ARCHER that simulated nuclear response procedures had alarmed Soviet intelligence officials, who thought it might be a prelude to a nuclear attack. The president could not believe that Moscow might be genuinely fearful of an American attack, but on 16 January he spoke of 'reducing the risk of war, and especially nuclear war' through arms control, while raising questions about Soviet compliance and possible evasions of previous treaties. Reagan's peace appeal to the Russians followed with charges of Soviet cheating provided the former governor of California with trump cards for the 1984 campaign that the Democrats found hard to top.

Subsequently, a series of reports to Congress claimed a variety of Soviet violations (and the Soviets responded with their own list of US evasions), most of which were 'grey-area' complaints. Moscow was guilty, however, of two significant violations – an uncompleted radar site, violating ABM terms, and a vast experimental biological warfare project (largely undiscovered until after the Cold War) violating the Biological Warfare Convention.

At the Reykjavik summit in October 1986, Reagan suggested the elimination of all ballistic missiles within 10 years. Secretary General Gorbachev immediately countered with the elimination of all Soviet and US strategic nuclear weapons within 10 years and restricting the Strategic Defense Initiative – Reagan's missile defence scheme, dubbed 'Star Wars' by the media (see the next chapter) – to an experimental stage for a decade. When Reagan refused to accept any limitations on his 'Star Wars' project, these radical arms-reduction proposals were dropped – much to the relief of US military leaders and NATO members and, undoubtedly, to senior Soviet marshals.

Nonetheless, there was a significant breakthrough at Reykjavik when Gorbachev agreed to American demands for on-site inspections. With the Limited Nuclear Test Ban and the SALT I pacts, Washington had settled for verification by national technical means – employing satellite reconnaissance, electronic monitoring, and other self-managed intelligence-gathering techniques. After Reykjavik, it was the Soviets who insisted on intrusive inspections, but the Pentagon and intelligence agencies began having second thoughts as they realized they did not want the Soviets prowling US defence plants. As Secretary of Defense Frank Carlucci admitted, 'verification has proven to be more complex than we thought it would be. The flip side of the coin is its application to us. The more we think about it, the more difficult it becomes.'

Shortly after Reykjavik, Gorbachev again surprised NATO and Washington leaders by accepting the US's 'zero-option' for an intermediate-range (INF) missile pact that required disproportionate Soviet reductions, including their missiles in Asia. On 8 December 1987, he and Reagan signed the INF treaty that included the first nuclear arms reductions and an elaborate US-Soviet on-site inspection system. Not until after the conclusion of the Cold War did Presidents George H. W. Bush and Gorbachev sign the complex 750-page START I treaty, in July 1991. This was the first agreement that called for significant cuts in strategic weaponry, as almost 50% of nuclear warheads carried on each power's ballistic missiles were to be eliminated. The treaty was to be in effect for 15 years and be renewable. It was a very promising moment in the annals of limiting the bomb.

Chapter 6
Star Wars

At the onset of the Cold War in the late 1940s, American officials
believed that the United States' sole possession of atomic bombs
would simply deter the Soviet Union from expanding further
into Western Europe or Asia. After the Soviets developed atomic
weapons and aircraft capable of delivering them over the North
Pole during the early 1950s, the United States accelerated its
efforts to obtain missiles capable of shooting down enemy
bombers. The advent of thermonuclear warheads by the late 1950s
and the deployment of nuclear-tipped intercontinental ballistic
missiles (ICBMs) by the early 1960s, spurred the search of both
superpowers for viable anti-ballistic missile defence systems
(ABM systems).

Both Washington and Moscow found themselves caught up in
an offensive and defensive arms race that threatened the stability
of the embryonic nuclear deterrence system. As the concept of
deterrence began to take hold, initial concerns arose as to whether
an anti-ballistic missile defence system would actually provide
much 'defence', and whether it was cost-effective. Eventually US
domestic politics, driven by partisanship and the threat of 'the axis
of evil', overcame previous concerns about costs and effectiveness
as President George W. Bush ordered deployment of an untested
ABM system in 2002.

Initial US missile defence projects

The United States' defensive missile programmes began in November 1944 when the US army contracted with the General Electric Company to investigate ways to protect American forces from Germany's V-2 rockets. Later, General Electric's research on ballistic missile defences was accelerated with the assistance of captured German documents and German scientists arriving in 1946. Within 12 months it had assembled and fired 100 V-2 missiles to obtain essential data about an offensive ballistic missile's trajectory and re-entry into the atmosphere. Research eventually led to the Nike-Ajax, the army anti-aircraft missile, in 1953, and Nike-Hercules, the army's follow-on anti-aircraft missile system, the next year.

Two Soviet developments in 1957 alarmed Americans and, at the same time, challenged their scientists to develop an anti-missile system. In August, the Soviets tested an intercontinental ballistic missile, and in October they startled the world by launching Sputnik I, the first orbiting artificial satellite. These events raised questions about the United States' vulnerability to a surprise nuclear attack – an impression that Soviet leaders were keen to foster, as they announced its rockets were able to reach any part of the globe. President Dwight Eisenhower created a high-level commission, led by Rowan Gaither, which recommended, among other things, the development of an anti-ballistic missile defence system that would protect the Strategic Air Command's missile bases.

Domestic politics and the desire to stabilize the nuclear environment played a major role in American and Soviet ABM decisions after the 1962 Cuban Missile Crisis. Members of Congress, alarmed at the United States' vulnerability during the 1962 crisis, urged the president to immediately deploy a national ABM system. The Soviets, meanwhile, upgraded their liquid-fuelled long-range missiles – which took considerable care and time to prepare for launch – with more dependable, quickly launched solid-fuel ICBMs. By 1967, the Soviets had an estimated 470 solid-fuel ICBMs, while the United States possessed 1,146, suggesting both superpowers possessed more than enough missiles to effectively deter each other. Unless, perhaps, one side possessed an effective national ballistic missile defence system.

President Lyndon Johnson's 24 January 1967 budget message to Congress indicated that the development of the promising Nike-X ABM system would continue, but that it was not yet ready to be deployed. The Nike-X was basically an army anti-ballistic missile system, linking multiple-array radar with an interceptor missile. Subsequently, however, the Chairman of the Joint Chiefs of Staff, General Earle Wheeler, told the House Appropriations Committee that the US should immediately deploy a light missile defence, but acknowledged that the Joint Chiefs preferred a heavy ABM city defence system for 'the highest density populated areas'. Wheeler insisted 'the Nike-X was ready for deployment'. Other prominent Americans, including the Committee for a Prudent Defense Policy, wanted a broad-based US ABM system deployed to meet the Soviet Golash ABM system's challenge to stability of deterrence.

Despite considerable pressure, Secretary of Defense Robert McNamara questioned the effectiveness of the Nike-X system and worried that ABM systems were becoming a destabilizing factor endangering the existing nuclear parity between US and Soviet Union. He urged President Johnson to go slow because there were two other, more cost-effective alternatives: (1) improvement of the United States' offensive capabilities; and (2) consultation with the Soviets about the possibility of limiting offensive and defensive strategic arms.

At the brief June 1967 summit meeting with President Lyndon Johnson at Glassboro, New Jersey, Premier Aleksei Kosygin insisted that the Soviet Union's projected defensive missile systems 'don't kill people. They protect them.' Moreover, he insisted, 'Defense is moral; offense is immoral.' Ironically, three and a half decades later, James M. Lindsay and Michael E. O'Hanlon argued 'a national security policy that deliberately leaves the American people vulnerable to attack when technology makes it possible to protect them is immoral and unacceptable. Not only does it fly in the face of common sense to leave the nation undefended, but it could hamstring America's role in the world.'

Without defences, proponents of ABMs believed governments hostile to the United States who possessed nuclear-tipped ballistic missiles might well believe they could threaten America's extensive worldwide interests and thus deter Washington from taking measures to protect them. Also, without an adequate missile defence the United States' allies might question Washington's willingness to honour its security pledges and thus lessen its global influence. Later, fears arose in the US that terrorist groups might obtain ballistic missiles with nuclear warheads to target American cities.

In contrast, opponents of ABM programmes questioned the high costs and effectiveness of projected US ballistic missile defences. They have also worried about the destabilizing impact of such anti-missile systems on relations with allies and adversaries. Would rival nations fear that the United States – should Washington believe the US to be impervious to retaliation – might flaunt its strategic arsenal as a means of pressuring them to conform to Washington's wishes or face serious consequences? Would US missile defences cause a fearful opponent to feel compelled to strike first, early in a crisis, with full force? Would such activity, in fact, impede strategic arms-limitation efforts? Would the next step be to place nuclear weapons in space? Would US missile defences renew the strategic nuclear arms race?

Thus, opponents contended that should a nationwide missile defence result in an enemy considering launching a first strike, in stimulating an arms race in outer space, or in the proliferation of ballistic missiles and weapons of mass destruction, Americans would find themselves with much reduced security. They repeatedly urged that strategic arms-control activities not be sacrificed in a dubious, costly quest for technological solutions or squandered in unilateral ventures.

Soviet missile defence projects

The United States' monopoly of the nuclear weapons in the late 1940s, and the possession of bombers to deliver them, prompted the Soviet Union to concentrate on defensive systems. In 1947, the Soviets began experimenting with anti-aircraft missiles modelled on Germany's World War II rockets and, eventually, on 25 May 1953, their V-300 missile and radar guidance system successfully shot down a TU-4 unmanned bomber. Six months later, the construction of an anti-aircraft missile defence system (S-5) began around Moscow to shield the city from up to 1,000 attacking bombers; in 1956 the defensive ring was designated to receive the Soviet's first anti-ballistic missile system (A-35 or 'Galosh') by November 1967. However, tests of its new S-350 interceptor missile indicated it could not cope with the US's new multiple-independently-targeted re-entry vehicle (MIRV). Each US ICBM re-entry vehicle (often referred to as a bus), could now carry several decoys and three or more individual nuclear-armed warheads.

Meanwhile, the Soviets decided in 1974 to develop the A-135 ABM system as a replacement for the A-35. The A-135 had been designed to counter either single or MIRVed ICBMs and was to have a two-tier defence capability. The first tier of interceptor missiles with A-350 launchers would attack ICBMs outside the atmosphere (exoatmospheric), while the second tier of

A-350 launchers would deal with ICBMs in the atmosphere (endoatmospheric). The first-tier system was confronted with the difficulty of locating and differentiating between decoys and warheads, the most serious problems confronting any anti-ballistic missile system. Following successful tests of the two-tier system at Sary Shagan in 1975 and 1976, the Minister of Defence authorized construction of seven A-135 sites around Moscow, beginning with the multipurpose Don–2N radar system in 1978 and hardened missile silos beginning in 1981 that were completed in November 1987. However, the A-135 system did not become fully operational until around 1997.

The Russians still have little confidence in the ability of their ABM systems to stop the penetration of ballistic missiles. Consequently, they have since the end of the Cold War concentrated on improving their ICBMs and equipping them with decoys to defeat any US ABM system.

The United States' unrestricted development of nuclear-tipped cruise missiles, which could be launched from bombers or submarines, confronted the Soviet Union with new threats. After launching, American cruise missiles could fly at low altitudes, enabling them to enter Soviet territory without being detected by the Soviet's existing radar, and allowing them to penetrate deeply into Soviet territory to destroy ICBMs in their silos.

To protect their ICBM silos and administrative and industrial sectors from cruise missiles, Soviet scientists between 1975 and 1980 sought to develop a theatre defence system employing a standardized multi-channel surface-to-air missile – the SAM-300 system. The S-300V could protect the Soviet army's ground units, while the S-300F defended naval ships, and the S-300P protected air defence forces. The S-300P systems had their equipment and launchers mounted on mobile trailer platforms connected by cables and given the name S-300PT. In 1980, the S-300PT system using the 5V55 surface-to-air missile was deployed around Moscow to supplement the A-135 system. The S-300PT system remained on station until 1985, when it was replaced by an upgraded SS-300PM mounted on self-propelled trailers designed to traverse almost any terrain and linked by radio-relays to command and control centres.

In 2005–6, the Russian air force began replacing its S-300P with the S-400 (NATO reporting name SA-20 Triumf) surface-to-air missile systems mounting an upgraded 48N6DM long-range interceptor designed to destroy aircraft, cruise missiles, and short- and medium-range ballistic missiles at ranges of up to 400 kilometres (250 miles). The S-400 has approximately 2.5 times the range of the S-300P, and twice the range of the US Patriot Advanced Capability-3 (PAC-3) system. Lightweight 9M96 interceptor missiles, with a range of about 120 kilometres (75 miles), will be mounted to counter low-flying targets. As *Jane's Missiles and Rockets* subsequently reported, eventually all 35 regiments will be equipped with the new system, which will be used to protect large population centres, as well as military and industrial complexes.

Moscow has been aggressively marketing the S-400 throughout Asia, Europe, and the Middle East. Between 2003 and 2004, China spent approximately $500 million on future S-400 systems. Additionally, Russia has offered the S-400 to the United Arab Emirates, and there is also speculation that Iran, a potential nuclear power, is currently seeking to acquire its own S-400 missiles. Once the S-400 completed its final tests and entered production, it was expected to become one of the most sought-after missile defence systems in the world. Yet as the US Patriot systems proved in two Gulf wars, the American and Russian systems still had deficiencies to deal with and could not guarantee that an enemy's cruise or short-range missile would be stopped.

First US ABM deployment

In September 1967, the beleaguered Johnson administration agreed to deploy a 'thin-line' Nike-X ABM system to protect the US from China's less potent nuclear missile threat, but made it clear the proposed ABM system would not effectively protect the US from a Soviet ICBM attack. By targeting China, the proposed Sentinel system left the door open for the Soviet Union to consider seriously the limitation or reduction of ABMs and ICBMs. It fell to the Nixon administration to undertake the actual deployment.

Shortly after his inauguration, Nixon announced on 14 March 1969 that: 'After a long study of all of the options available, I have concluded that the Sentinel program previously adopted should be substantially modified.' The new ABM system would 'not provide defense for our cities' because 'I found that there is no way that we can adequately defend our cities without an unacceptable loss of life.' Therefore, in 1970, he authorized the new Safeguard system to protect up to 12 Minuteman III ICBM sites at Malstrom AFB, Montana, and at Grand Forks AFB, North Dakota, in order to preserve a credible deterrent.

Nixon chose not to mention the enhancement of the Safeguard ABM system, which increased the number of ABM interceptors to protect Minuteman III ICBM sites and altered Sentinel's radar range to cover the continental United States. Kissinger's memoirs indicated that the extended radar coverage would create 'a better base for rapid expansion' of ICBMs site defences if needed in the future. (Soviet scientists correctly anticipated that the omitted data about radar coverage was part of the Safeguard plan.)

Because of Safeguard's technical limitations, the House of Representatives voted on 2 October 1975 to deactivate the single ABM site (instead of the planned 12) at Grand Forks, North Dakota, after spending $6 billion – some four months after it became operational. This action followed the realization that Safeguard's large phased-array radars provided easy targets for Soviet missiles and, additionally, that when nuclear warheads on the Spartan and Sprint missiles detonated, the explosions blinded the radar system.

The 1972 ABM Treaty

Meanwhile, the first steps towards US–Soviet negotiations on missile defence systems began in 1964 when William Foster, US director of the Arms Control and Disarmament Agency, explored the possibility of negotiations to ban or place limits on the anti-ballistic missile systems with Anatoly Dobrynin, the Soviet Union's ambassador to the United States. Moscow did not act on these initial American suggestions, according to Dobrynin, because members of the Politburo could not agree on whether to negotiate with Washington. On 10 August 1968, the Kremlin finally decided to begin discussions to limit or eliminate offensive and defensive strategic weapons. Unfortunately, these planned talks were sidetracked on 24 August, when Soviet forces intervened in Czechoslovakia.

Strategic arms discussions that began in Helsinki, Finland, on 17 November 1969, found American delegates pressing their concern, both formally and privately, that ballistic missile defence systems endangered current deterrence stability. Early in the talks, the Soviets indicated a willingness to limit ABM deployment 'to geographically and numerically low limits'. Confronted with unresolved issues regarding strategic offensive forces, it was finally agreed in 1971 to seek separate agreements.

During late August 1971, American delegate Harold Brown was asked to clarify the United States' 'understanding of the notion of "development" and of practical application of limitations'. After checking with his superiors, Brown carefully responded that:

By 'development' we have in mind that stage in the evolution of a weapon system which follows research (in research we include the activities of conceptual design and laboratory testing) and which precedes full-scale testing. The development stage, though often overlapping with research, is usually associated with the construction and testing of one or more prototypes of the weapon system or its major components. In our view, it is entirely logical and practical to prohibit the development – in this sense – of those systems whose testing and deployment are prohibited.

Unknowingly, Brown had provided a definition that would be employed in the 1980s by opponents of President Ronald Reagan's 'Star Wars' system to reinterpret the 1972 ABM pact.

By the fall of 1971, the Soviet and American delegates, meeting at Geneva, agreed on the basic elements of Article V of the ABM Treaty that read: 'Each Party undertakes not to develop, test, or deploy ABM systems or components which are sea-based, air-based, space-based, or mobile land-based.' Fixed land-based systems were defined in Article II as 'a system to counter strategic ballistic missiles or their elements in flight trajectory, currently consisting of' ABM interceptors, launchers, and radars. The phrase 'currently consisting of' indicated that the treaty was to cover all systems – current and future.

The Soviets exercised a persistent inquisitiveness regarding 'exotic' systems, partly because for months American delegates were prevented – by their military chiefs – from using lasers as an example. The Soviets were aware of America's laser programme and, in fact, hoped to employ their own large lasers in anti-missile experiments. Eventually, Soviet probing and, perhaps, their hope to glean information about the US exotic programme, gave way to an agreement to ban the deployment of fixed-based exotic ABMs. In the Agreed Statement D of the ABM Treaty, a footnote stated that:

... the Parties agree that in the event ABM systems based on other physical principles and including components capable of substituting for ABM interceptor missiles, ABM launchers, or ABM radars are created in the future, specific limitations on such systems and their components would be subject to discussion ... and agreement.

The ABM Treaty limited each side to two ABM sites (later reduced to one) separated by no less than 1,300 kilometres (800 miles), to keep them from overlapping. Consequently, each of the two permitted sites was restricted to specific areas and could only provide limited coverage. The treaty clearly prohibited the establishment of a nationwide ballistic missile defence system. At Moscow, on 22 May 1972, the terms of the ABM Treaty agreement were finalized and signed.

Reagan's Star Wars proposal

Following a Pentagon's Defense Science Board review, the White House concluded in October 1981 that its 'ballistic missile technology [was] not at the stage' where it can provide 'defenses against Soviet missiles'. This finding, according to Ronald Reagan's biographer, Lou Cannon, did not lessen the president's 'vision of nuclear apocalypse and his deeply rooted conviction that the weapons that could cause this hell on earth should be abolished'. Moreover, Reagan was morally opposed to the US's 20-year-old deterrence doctrine, 'assured destruction'.

In early 1983, President Reagan was preparing a speech in support of another increase in the Defense Department's budget for fiscal year 1984 that was being challenged by a grass-roots nuclear freeze movement. He rejected the first draft because it repeated previous justifications. Rather than rehash old themes, Reagan urged his national security advisor, Robert C. McFarlane, to develop something new to counteract the message of nuclear freeze proponents. Public opinion polls in 1982 and January 1983 revealed that 66% of Americans believed Reagan was not performing well in promoting arms control, and 70% supported a freeze on nuclear weapons production as a first step to eliminate all nuclear warheads. A congressional debate on a nuclear freeze, which threatened increases in military expenditures, was scheduled for the end of March 1983.

Senator Malcolm Wallop (R-WY), Lt General Daniel O. Graham (retired), and physicist Edward Teller of the University of California Lawrence Livermore Laboratories had been lobbying the Pentagon and Congress from 1979 to 1982 for increased funding of missile defence projects. They sought support for such concepts as nuclear and chemically based lasers, orbiting space-based battle stations using lasers, and an improved air force space-aircraft. In February 1981, Secretary of Defense Caspar Weinberger told the Senate Committee on Armed Forces that the US might be able to 'deploy MX [missiles] in fixed silos protected by ABMs'. However, none of these advocates of anti-missile systems was directly involved in preparing Reagan's March 1983 speech.

On 11 February 1983, Reagan and the Joint Chiefs of Staff discussed the Pentagon's list of five options to deal with current strategic weaponry. One option was Chief of Naval Operations, Admiral James Watkins's proposed missile defence system. He argued that a forward strategic ballistic missile defence would 'move battles from our shores and skies'. Such battles would be 'moral' and palatable to the American people because a missile defence system would protect Americans, 'not just avenge them', after a Soviet attack. It seemed realistic, Watkins concluded, to have a long-range programme to 'develop systems that would defeat a missile attack'. Reagan gravitated to Watkins's missile defence idea as a way to alleviate his moral aversion to the reality of nuclear deterrence.

Meanwhile, McFarlane and the president's science advisor, George Keyworth II, were drafting Reagan's speech scheduled for 23 March. Keyworth initially opposed inclusion of a missile defence plan, but reluctantly withdrew his objections after McFarlane informed him that inclusion of the proposed missile defence system was a political, not a scientific, decision.

According to Reagan's autobiography, he received a final draft of the speech on 22 March and that night 'did a lot of rewriting. Much of it was to change bureaucratese [sic] into people talk.' In its finished form, his speech began with a lengthy section designed to persuade Congress to approve a significant increase in funds for fiscal year 1984 to continue the US military build-up. As his speech drew to a close, Reagan told his audience of recent discussions about missile defence with the Joint Chiefs of Staff. Then, after noting that the nation's security previously depended on nuclear deterrence, Reagan continued:

> Let me share with you a vision of the future which offers hope. It is that we embark on a program to counter the awesome Soviet military threat with measures that are defensive. ... What if free people could live secure in the knowledge that their security did not rest on the threat of instant U.S. retaliation to deter a Soviet attack, that we could intercept and destroy strategic ballistic missiles before they reached our own soil or that of our allies?

Acknowledging this would be a formidable undertaking, he suggested that as current technology offered promise, it was time to begin creating a defensive shield.

> I call upon the scientific community in this country, who gave us nuclear weapons, ... to give us the means of rendering these weapons impotent and obsolete. Tonight, consistent with our obligations of the ABM Treaty ... , I'm taking an important first step. I am directing a comprehensive and intensive effort to define

a long-term research and development program to begin to achieve
our ultimate goal of eliminating the threat posed by strategic
nuclear missiles.

The president's proposal was officially titled the Strategic Defense
Initiative (SDI) in January 1984, while critics dubbed it 'Star
Wars'.

The response to Reagan's proposal was decidedly mixed.
Undersecretary of Defense Richard Delauer, who endorsed
funding ABM research, objected to it being subjected to such
a 'half-baked political travesty'. When cornered by a reporter,
Minority Whip Robert Michel of Illinois said the speech may
have been 'a bit of overkill'. *Time* magazine's lead story after
the speech suggested Reagan's proposal was representative of
a 'video-game vision', and its cover pictured Reagan against a
background of space weapons resembling a Buck Rogers comic
strip about the 25th century. Within a week, however, Reagan's
missile defence proposal had disappeared because it no longer was
considered newsworthy, and the public's attention shifted to more
immediate issues. Indeed, during the 1984 election campaign,
Reagan did not mention missile defence, even though Democratic
candidate Walter Mondale denounced it as a dangerous hoax
costing American taxpayers billions of dollars, speeding up the
arms race while providing no real protection to the American
people.

Taking the SDI proposal seriously, the Defense Department
created two expert panels in the spring of 1983 – the Fletcher and
Hoffman groups – to examine possible missile defence systems.
James C. Fletcher, former director of the National Aeronautics
and Space Agency, headed a 65-member panel – 53 of whom had
direct financial interests in SDI research – asked to plan a missile
defence. In early 1984, the panel recommended that all research
aspects of SDI should be accelerated to reach a decision on
deploying a missile defence system in the early 1990s.

The Fletcher panel proposed a layered-interceptor missile defence system. The first layer involved SDI sensors detecting ICBMs leaving their silos and the immediate launching of missile interceptors to attack the enemy missiles in their boost phase. The second layer of US interceptors would seek to destroy enemy warheads in the post-boost, or bus deployment, phase. The third layer of interceptors would look for any deployed enemy warheads during a midcourse phase before they entered the atmosphere. Finally, a fourth layer of interceptors would sort out surviving warheads from the decoys and debris during the terminal phase and destroy them.

Destroying enemy ICBMs in the brief initial boost phase of three to five minutes would provide the best opportunity for reducing the number of incoming warheads. After the boost phase passed, the post-boost vehicle ('bus') would continue to carry the warheads and decoys. The post-boost phase would take six to ten minutes to reach its apogee of some 750 miles above the earth, during which time a second US layer of interceptors would try to find and destroy the bus. This is the next best time to intercept the nuclear warheads. At its apogee, the bus would adjust its trajectory and release up to ten nuclear warheads, plus numerous decoys, all of which would begin descending towards selected targets on earth.

The third layer of missile defence comes into play during the midcourse phase after the bus releases the warheads and decoys and before these objects re-enter the earth's atmosphere. This layer gives the US missile defence system its greatest amount of time, perhaps up to 20 minutes, to locate and destroy the incoming warheads that are heading towards their targets. US interceptors, however, may be diverted from the warheads by decoys and space debris that they could mistake for enemy warheads.

The final missile defence phase begins when warheads and decoys re-enter the atmosphere about 60 miles above the earth. During this phase, interceptors have only tens of seconds to hit warheads before they reach their target. The one advantage for defensive missiles at this stage is that the warhead's skin is heated by friction, while decoys, presumably lighter-weight, cool down after they separate from the warheads.

For the ballistic missile defence system to qualify for deployment, it should effectively fulfil three tasks. First, the system must be able to detect and identify enemy targets, that is, distinguish among ICBM booster rockets, warheads, decoys, and debris. Second, the system's tracking devices must be able to locate and plot the trajectory of a target in order to guide an interceptor missile to its target. Finally, a defence system must be able to assess the damage caused by the defensive weapon to assure the destruction of the booster rocket, bus, or warhead. This is necessary so that defenders can determine whether they must launch additional interceptors.

Obviously, such a comprehensive ballistic missile defence posed a most daunting challenge to the scientists and technicians who were to undertake the necessary research to develop and test the complex parts of the system. It also required large increases in the Defense Department's budget, much larger than the estimates initially offered by the Reagan administration.

Meanwhile, arms negotiator and diplomat Paul Nitze had presented a three-part formula that any SDI system would need to meet before it could be considered for deployment. The 'Nitze criteria', as it was known, stated that the anti-missile system should: (1) be effective; (2) be able to survive against a direct attack; and (3) be cost-effective at the margin – that is, less costly to increase your defence than your opponent's costs to increase their offensive against it. Nitze's formula was adopted as National

6. The 'Star Wars' defence system

Security Directive No. 172 on 30 May 1985, prompting some at the Pentagon to fear that stressing cost-effectiveness would essentially kill the programme. Others, such as Robert McNamara, doubted that the Reagan administration planned to adhere to the cost portion of the criteria.

At the same time, a Future Security Strategy Study team – with 17 of its 24 members future SDI contractors – chaired by Fred S. Hoffman, also assessed the nation's strategic defences. In early 1984, the Hoffman study offered a more realistic appraisal of the SDI's time frame. Rather than anticipating a possible ABM deployment in the early 1990s, Hoffman's team concluded that a perfect defence might 'take a long time and may prove to be unattainable in a practical sense against a Soviet effort to counter the defense'.

For more than a decade, the traditional interpretation of the ABM Treaty was seen as prohibiting any development and testing of a space-based ABM system. But in October 1985, Nitze persuaded Secretary of State George Schultz to accept a 'broad' interpretation of the 1972 Treaty that would permit research and development of space-based weapons. Other administration hard-liners – who desired to scrap the ABM Treaty – sought instead to broaden the new interpretation further to permit testing of space weapons.

On 6 October, National Security Adviser Robert McFarlane told NBC's 'Meet the Press' that the 1972 ABM Treaty allowed development and research of a missile defence system that involved 'new physical concepts'. He also argued that the treaty permitted the testing of exotic systems and technologies – presumably lasers and particle beams.

The State Department's legal adviser, Abraham D. Sofaer, argued that the classified ABM treaty negotiation record and treaty provisions showed its language to be ambiguous and that the record of Senate ratification supported the broader view. He also claimed, without providing any substantiation, that the Soviet Union never accepted a ban on mobile ABM systems or on exotic technologies. (Sofaer eventually had to acknowledge that the ratification records did not support the broad interpretation and blamed the errors on his staff's 'young lawyers'.)

The administration's efforts to broaden the interpretation of the 1972 ABM Treaty provoked a major executive-legislative disagreement. Warning the president that any actions in violation of the traditional interpretation of the pact would cause 'a constitutional confrontation of profound dimensions', Senator Sam Nunn (D-GA) launched a series of studies of the reinterpretation that concluded Sofaer's legal reasoning was in 'serious error'. Joined by Senator Carl Levin (D-MI), Nunn sponsored an amendment to the defence authorization bill prohibiting any SDI testing that challenged the traditional interpretation of the ABM Treaty prohibitions. Following a sharp partisan debate and an extended Republican filibuster, a modified version of the Nunn-Levin wording was approved in late 1987.

The Republicans won control of the House and Senate in 1994 and attributed victory to their 'Contract with America' that among other issues reflected how deeply the commitment to a nationwide missile defence had become enmeshed in the party's political ideology. It called for deploying a 'cost-effective, operational anti-ballistic missile defence system' as early as possible to protect the United States 'against ballistic missile threats (for example, accidental or unauthorized launches or Third World attacks) ... '. Moreover, the contract insisted that the ABM Treaty was 'a Cold War relic that does not meet the future defence needs of the United States. ... It is a moral imperative that US strategic defenses be expanded and that the Clinton administration not yield to Russian demands that Americans remain defenseless in the face of potential nuclear aggression....' During subsequent years, Republican legislators unsuccessfully sought to mandate deployment of a national missile defence system.

The Republicans appointed an independent commission in November 1996 to 'Assess the Ballistic Missile Threat'. Under the direction of future Secretary of Defense David Rumsfeld, the Rumsfeld commission's declassified Executive Summary emphasized that: 'The newer ballistic missile-equipped nations [North Korea, Iran, and Iraq] ... would be able to inflict major destruction on the US within about five years of a decision to acquire such a capability (10 years in the case of Iraq).' North Korea and Iran, who the commission thought to be developing weapons of mass destruction, were alleged to have put 'a high priority on threatening US territory, and each is even now pursuing advanced ballistic missile capabilities to pose a direct threat to US territory'.

Greg Thielmann, formerly of the State Department's Bureau of Intelligence and Research, found 'Rumsfeld's view on ballistic missiles often ignored the carefully considered views of [intelligence] professionals in favor of highly unlikely worst-case scenarios that posited an imminent threat to the United States and prompted a military, rather than diplomatic, response.' This was not surprising.

George W. Bush and ABM deployment

Not long after being inaugurated as president in January 2001, George W. Bush undertook to fulfil his campaign promise to actively pursue a national missile defence system. After the 11 September 2001 terrorist attacks, Bush insisted that a missile defence system was necessary for American security. To remove all limitations on research, development, and testing of missile defences, he announced on 13 December 2001 that the United States had given Moscow the required six months' notice of its intention to withdraw from the 1972 ABM Treaty.

A year later, in December 2002, President Bush instructed the Defense Department to deploy the initial elements of a strategic missile defence system. The modest deployment included 20 ground-based midcourse missile defence (GMD) interceptors and 20 sea-based Aegis ballistic missile defence interceptors positioned on three vessels. Also included were an unspecified quantity of Patriot PAC-3 missiles and upgraded radar systems to help locate potential targets. The PAC-3 missiles and the sea-based interceptors were intended to protect against short- and medium-range ballistic missiles. Only the 20 GMD interceptors – 16 to be placed in Alaska and 4 located at Vandenberg Air Force Base – were designed to protect against long-range ballistic missiles. Informed observers fully understood that the intercept tests of the rudimentary GMD intercepting rockets had been carefully scripted with modest challenges; even the 'successful' ones did not resemble real-world conditions. A reliable ABM system appeared still to be years away.

Further considerations

Among several remaining contentious considerations are three questions that deserve further comment: (1) Will a missile defence system provide the best defence against rogue states and terrorists?; (2) Has the political partisanship that drove the deployment decision become a faith-based commitment?; and (3) What will the missile defences cost?

Most Americans agree that possession of an effective missile defence would be desirable; however, many sceptics are concerned that the precipitous deployment of unproven systems, at substantial expense, could fall far short of providing the desired shield. Several analysts have contended that given the United States' enormous nuclear arsenal and global delivery capabilities, no nation would allow the launch of a ballistic missile from its territory because such hostile action would result in immediate American retaliation and annihilation of the offending state.

A much more likely threat to the United States, according to these specialists, is that foreign terrorists, if they chose to use weapons of mass destruction, would employ a ship or truck to carry them to American soil – not long-range ballistic missiles which are complicated to build, deploy, and launch with accuracy. Thus America's greatest threat, in the words of one commentator, is not from rogue states, but from stateless rogues.

Ever since President Reagan's SDI speech, the heated debates and demands for immediate deployment of a missile shield can be traced to the domestic political environment. So-called 'conservative' Republicans became increasingly strident in their determination to terminate the 1972 ABM Treaty and to deploy an anti-missile system. This commitment bordered on theological cant, appeared in official party documents, and brooked little or no compromise. Moreover, Republican demand for deployment paid little attention to time-proven procedures for developing weapons systems, for concerns of various technological deficiencies of the anti-missile systems, for the financial costs or the impact of deployment upon broader foreign policy considerations.

A third consideration is that past research and development activities have consumed more than $120 billion, and costs will continue to mount with the decision to deploy unproven technology. The head of the Missile Defense Agency (MDA), General Ronald Kadish, illustrated the administration's lack of concern regarding the costs of what many regard as premature deployment, because he proposed to 'Test, fix. Test, fix. Test, fix.' While this is the usual process in the experimental stage, it becomes more expensive once 'operational' units are fielded.

In its June 2003 report, the General Accounting Office (GAO) questioned the wisdom of the Pentagon's push for deploying a limited missile defence at the expense of ignoring the proven approach to developing weapons systems and for employing a 'test, fix' policy. Consequently, the GAO warned that the administration was risking the deployment of costly, ineffective anti-missile systems.

The MDA has estimated that the deployment would probably cost an additional 50 billion dollars. The GAO, however, emphasized that this sum only related to research and development expenses. It did not include the cost of production, operations, and maintenance that earlier Pentagon figures estimated could be nearly another $150 billion. The GAO urged the Pentagon to consider preparing a comprehensive estimate of missile defence costs and that it should begin budgeting for these expenditures. Failure to do so could result in the Defense Department being forced to shift funds from other weapons programmes to meet the costs of building and deploying the missile defence system.

Forecasting the costs of a layered-missile defence system is quite daunting. However, when the Economists Allied for Arms Reduction added up the Pentagon's own estimates for all of the elements of the various phases of the Bush administration's projects, including operating the systems for 20 years, they found it totalled a trillion dollars, maybe a trillion and a half. In a world in which the global strategic nuclear environment is rapidly changing, that may not even be enough.

EARLY US MISSILE DEFENCE SYSTEMS
(**a selective list of American missile programmes**)

PROJECT	DATE	RESEARCH AND PURPOSE
THUMPER	1944	Army research seeks protection from V-2 type rockets, leads to BAMBI (Ballistic Missile Boost Intercept), cancelled in 1961
NIKE	1945	Army launches research for anti-aircraft defence
GAPA	1947	Air force seeks Ground to Air Pilotless Aircraft, integrated in 1949 with THUMPER to hit and kill ballistic missiles

BUMBLEBEE	1947	Navy seeks surface-to-air missile, leads to TALOS
NIKE-AJAX	1953	Army anti-aircraft missile
NIKE-HERCULES	1954	Army anti-aircraft system
WIZARD	1955	Air force's anti-ballistic missile, eventually shifts to offensive missiles
NIKE-ZEUS	1956	Army anti-ballistic missiles system, links radar with interceptor rocket
TALOS	1958	Eventually becomes POLARIS submarine-launched ballistic missile (SLBM)
NIKE-ZEUS	1960	Army urges deployment to protect military bases, leads to NIKE-X
NIKE-X	1963	Multiple-array radar (ZMAR) and Sprint missile added to system
SENTINEL	1968	Designated as SENTINEL, NIKE-X to be deployed nationwide against China
SENTINEL	1969	Becomes SAFEGUARD and to be deployed at ICBM North Dakota/ Montana silos
SAFEGUARD	1975	SAFEGUARD becomes operational
SAFEGUARD	1976	Congress orders SAFEGUARD shut down

SOVIET URBAN AIR DEFENCE SYSTEMS

MOSCOW

A-25	1953	Anti-bomber defence uses V-300 surface-to-air missile
A-35	1958	Construction begins on GALOSH* system – planned to protect from ICBMs by 1967 using V-1000 missile
	1962	S-350 interceptor added to operate outside the atmosphere but it fails to counteract MIRVs
	1967	Work stopped on GALOSH due to ineffective testing and Moscow is defended only by ALDAN system of TU-126 fighter aircraft
	1975	A-350 interceptor upgrades against MIRVs
A-135	1978	System upgraded gradually
	1980	5V55 provide protection for air defence units
	1992	Has replaced A-35

LENINGRAD

	1961	Uses S-500 (GRIFFIN*) interceptors with single-stage SAM launcher – abandoned 1963
	1963	S-200 (GAMMON*) interceptor with two-stage SAM launcher

Nuclear Weapons

1970	S-200V VOLGA increases range and adds ABM capabilities
1974	S-200D VEGA – upgrade of S-200V is abandoned after amended 1972 ABM Treaty limits each party to one site

*US designation

Chapter 7
Nuclear weapons in the age of terrorism

We conclude our analysis of nuclear weapons with a deceptively simple question: Does the spread of nuclear weapons make the world safer or more dangerous? Most people usually have an instinctive reply to this question: Of course, it makes things more dangerous. How could it not? It might seem surprising, therefore, that not all nuclear analysts agree, and the debate remains unresolved. Like so many of the issues relating to nuclear weapons, the debate is built largely on speculation and ambiguous historical experience. Nuclear weapons remain attractive to insecure or ambitious states. In regional rivalries such as the subcontinent, East Asia, and the Middle East, the bomb still has influence. Whatever else one has to say – and presumably not much has been left unsaid about the nuclear strategy of the past six decades – nuclear status still imparts extraordinary prestige and power. The nine current members of the nuclear weapon club still possess about 27,000 operational nuclear weapons of various types between them. At least another 15 countries have on hand enough highly enriched uranium for a nuclear weapon.

Since 1945, many influential voices have expressed alarm that the spread of nuclear weapons will inevitably lead to world destruction. So far, that prediction has not been proved right. But is that because of effective efforts to stop the spread of nuclear weapons, or, to borrow a phrase from former Secretary of State

Dean Acheson, after the Cuban Missile Crisis, just 'plain dumb luck'?

Nuclear proliferation remains urgent not just because of the risk of a terrorist organization getting its hands on nuclear weapons, but because the proliferation of weapons necessarily means a proliferation of nuclear deterrents. Nuclear weapons have long been a force multiplier, able to make up for imbalances in conventional military power. Paradoxically, then, the unassailable lead of the United States in military power and technology might actually invite other nations to acquire the bomb as a way to influence or even deter American foreign policy initiatives. The lesson of the first Gulf War, one Indian general was reported as saying, is that you do not go to war with the United States without the bomb, the 2003 invasion of Iraq serving as yet another glossy advertisement of the protective power of a nuclear arsenal. This is not a new development. It is, in fact, a lesson American policymakers have been concerned about for some time, and one for which no easy solution seems likely. Bill Clinton's Secretary of Defense, Les Aspin, outlined the problem in December 1993:

> During the Cold War, our principal adversary had conventional forces in Europe that were numerically superior. For us, nuclear weapons were the equalizer. The threat to use them was present and was used to compensate for our smaller numbers of conventional forces. Today, nuclear weapons can still be the equalizer against superior conventional forces. But today it is the United States that has unmatched conventional military power, and it is our potential adversaries who may attain nuclear weapons.

Accordingly, Aspin concluded, the United States could wind up being the equalized. To take an earlier example, John F. Kennedy acknowledged in the wake of the Cuban Missile Crisis that even a small number of nuclear weapons could deter even the most powerful states.

A central element of the proliferation debate revolves around the perceived effectiveness of nuclear deterrence. If deterrence works reliably, as optimists argue, then there is presumably less to be feared in the spread of nuclear weapons. But if nuclear deterrence does not work reliably, pessimists maintain, more nuclear weapons states will presumably lead not just to a more complicated international arena but a far more dangerous one.

Some analysts have made a compelling case that the fear of nuclear proliferation, or the spread of nuclear weapons, has been exaggerated. Some go even further and argue that proliferation may actually increase global stability. It is an argument peculiar to nuclear weaponry, as it does not apply and is not made with regard to other so-called weapons of mass destruction such as chemical and biological weapons. Nuclear weapons are simply so destructive, this school of thought argues, that using them is such a high bar that it would be madness itself to launch against a nuclear-armed foe. Put another way, nuclear states should know better than to fight wars with each other. The argument that proliferation is not necessarily a dire threat has been made in expansions both lateral – to other countries – and vertical – in the growth of nuclear stockpiles. 'Since 1945', remarked Michael Mandelbaum, 25 years ago, 'the more nuclear weapons each has accumulated, the less likely, on the whole, it has seemed that either side would use them'. Others have made similar arguments. Kenneth Waltz maintains, for example, that nuclear weapons preserve an 'imperfect peace' on the subcontinent between India and Pakistan. Responding to reports that all Pentagon war games involving India and Pakistan always end in a nuclear exchange, Waltz argues that 'Has everyone in that building forgotten that deterrence works precisely because nuclear states fear that conventional military engagements may escalate to the nuclear level, and therefore they draw back from the brink?'

It was an idea frequently debated during the Cold War. French military strategist General Pierre Gallois observed in 1960 that the path to greater stability lay in the increased proliferation. 'Few people are able to grasp that precisely because the new weapons have a destructive power out of all proportion to even the highest stakes, they impose a far more stable balance than the world has known in the past', he said. 'Nor is it any easier to make people realize that the more numerous and terrible the retaliatory weapons possessed by both sides, the surer the peace ... and that it is actually more dangerous to limit nuclear weapons than to let them proliferate.' Gallois made this argument in the context of justifying the French bomb and increasing NATO nuclear capabilities. 'These', Gallois concluded, 'are the realities of our time.'

Notwithstanding a few notable proponents of the 'proliferation equals more security' argument, the weight of opinion is mainly on the other side of the ledger, heightened, especially since 9/11, that the spread of nuclear weapons is a bad thing – a very bad thing, in fact. The issues driving nuclear-armed states and even terrorist groups are no longer just political; we have also seen the obsessiveness of religious fundamentalism, which does not seem amenable either to diplomacy or humanitarian restraint. Indeed, since 9/11 the 'rules' have changed and experts suggest that there are at least some terrorists who do want to inflict mass casualties. In this context, nuclear terrorism not only represents an effort to intimidate and coerce, but also poses a critical threat to states and peoples around the world.

Political scientist Scott Sagan has also highlighted the ways in which organizations and communications can fail; for example, rather than being anomalies, accidents should be seen as an inherent part of organizations. When nuclear weapons are thrown into the mix, the risk of catastrophic accidents becomes inevitable. Moreover, Sagan holds the view that a fundamental level of risk is inherent in all nuclear weapons organizations regardless of nationality or region. Clearly, it is an element that compounds the problem of nuclear weapons in regions still embroiled by centuries-old religious, cultural, and ethnic tensions. All of these elements combine in a barely controllable milieu of states' nuclear weapons policy, a disaster waiting to happen.

Halting the spread of nuclear weapons

This invariably leads us to our second, essential question: How can a nation – or a community of nations – prevent the spread of nuclear weapons? Since the question was first raised during the closing stages of World War II, a wide range of answers have been given and tried, ranging from the legislative, through international norms and treaties, and even preventive military action. None has proved entirely satisfactory.

Whereas the Baruch Plan equated controlling the atom and disarmament (discussed in Chapter 3), President Dwight D. Eisenhower managed to separate the two in his 1953 proposal known as 'Atoms for Peace'. The focus of the proposal was on stopping the spread of nuclear weapons, not on disarmament. In a speech to the United Nations on 8 December 1953, Eisenhower called for a renewed emphasis on peaceful uses of atomic energy and on providing commercial incentives for reaping the benefits of atomic energy. The price was that all fissile material would be placed under the custody of a UN agency. Again, the initiative met with mixed success. On the plus side, it contributed directly to the establishment of the International Atomic Energy Agency (IAEA), in July 1957, charged with monitoring and encouraging the safe use of nuclear technology for peaceful purposes, while acting as an international, neutral watchdog of nuclear weapons transfers and developments. The Vienna-based IAEA, a United Nations-affiliated organization with 137 member countries, has played an important role in recent years, but its power depends heavily on international political tides. On the negative side, a few nations, including India, chose to use the Atoms for Peace project to establish their own nuclear weapons programmes.

In the 1950s and 1960s, while the US, the Soviet Union, Great Britain, and France built their nuclear arsenal, frequent estimates of the future size of the nuclear-armed community centred on two-dozen states. But with the People's Republic of China's initial nuclear test in October 1964, a worried White House and Kremlin hastily put forth proposals to restrict the spread of nuclear weapons. In the Eighteen Nation Disarmament Committee, which had been discussing this matter, non-aligned members argued that a non-proliferation treaty must not simply divide the world into nuclear 'haves' and 'have-nots', but must balance obligations. The Non-Proliferation Treaty (NPT) was signed in 1968 after the Americans and the Soviets reluctantly agreed 'to pursue obligations in good faith' to halt the arms race 'at the earliest possible date' (the fig leaf they hid behind) and to seek 'a treaty on general and complete disarmament under strict effective international control'. Questionable adherence to this pledge annoyed non-nuclear nations at subsequent NPT review conferences only to draw renewed, feeble pledges from the superpowers.

Nevertheless, the Non-Proliferation Treaty became the cornerstone of a loosely structured non-proliferation regime. The IAEA established international inspections and safeguards aimed at preventing nuclear materials being diverted to military uses. During 1974 and 1975, a Nuclear Suppliers Group was established in London to further ensure that nuclear materials, equipment, and technology would not be used in weapons production. Various Nuclear Weapons Free Zones meanwhile extended the non-proliferation regime to Latin America (1967), the South Pacific (1996), Africa (1996), Southeast Asia (1997), and Central Asia (2002), while a Comprehensive Nuclear Test Ban Treaty, which the US Senate has refused to ratify, rounded out the regime. For all its faults, the NPT stands out as the high-water mark of multilateral global efforts to establish an enforceable regime to curb the further spread of nuclear weapons.

By the time the NPT was signed, the nuclear club already had five members: the United States, the Soviet Union, the United Kingdom, France, and China, who greeted each new addition meeting with varying degrees of concern. American policymakers engaged in serious discussion against both the Soviet and Chinese nuclear programmes before each successfully exploded its first atomic device in 1949 and 1964, respectively. The Indian Government of Prime Minister Indira Gandhi seriously considered, but ultimately rejected, plans for preventive military attacks on Pakistan's nuclear facilities in the early 1980s. Israel, not a signatory to the treaty, actually carried out a military strike against an Iraqi nuclear power facility on 7 June 1981, at Osirak. Less aggressive measures have also had a mixed record of success. American efforts to thwart the British nuclear programme consisted mainly of cutting off the flow of information and materials to their erstwhile atomic partner. The French were in point of fact actively discouraged from developing an independent nuclear option and offers were made for a European nuclear force instead. None of these efforts was decisive.

Not every nuclear and prospective nuclear power has regarded the NPT and its subsequent indefinite renewal in 1995 positively. After all, the NPT is specifically designed to freeze the status quo. The leading nuclear states party to the treaty naturally regarded this as a positive arrangement because it preserved their status while retaining their freedom with respect to modernizing their own nuclear arsenals, which they have clearly done. But other countries such as India, not a signatory to the treaty, saw it as exclusionary on the part of the established nuclear powers and bristled at what it perceived to be the nuclear double standards of the West, Russia and China. For, according to former Indian defence minister K. C. Pant, 'We very seriously proposed a 15-year plan for the phased elimination of nuclear weapons. However, after the NPT was extended "in perpetuity", it was apparent the big powers had no intention of shedding their nuclear arsenal.'

India may well have gone nuclear because of double standards and the wish to be taken seriously.

Disarmament critics also argue that under the NPT, the nuclear powers should not be expanding their nuclear arsenals but rather moving towards total nuclear disarmament. Article VI of the treaty is clear: 'Each of the Parties to the Treaty undertakes to pursue negotiations in good faith on effective measures relating to cessation of the nuclear arms race at an early date and to nuclear disarmament, and on a treaty on general and complete disarmament under strict and effective international control.' Moreover, continue critics, what possible purpose could nuclear weapons serve in the war on international terrorism? And could not the expense of modernizing nuclear forces be better put to use?

Typically, and in defence of his government's decision to update and replace the United Kingdom's Trident nuclear weapons system, former British Prime Minister Tony Blair responded to his opposition by pointing out that the NPT did not commit member states to total disarmament but rather to negotiations on effective measures and that his government had fulfilled this pledge. It had, in fact, cut its nuclear weapons explosive capacity by 70% since the end of the Cold War, given up bombs carried by strategic aircraft, and reduced the operational readiness of its four Vanguard submarines, each carrying 16 US-supplied Trident ballistic missiles equipped with up to three warheads. In any case, only one submarine was on patrol at any one time and would require several days' notice to fire. Nonetheless, there was considerable resistance. On 24 February 2007, the national 'No Trident' demonstration brought up to 100,000 protestors to the streets of London to demand the government reverse its plans to build a new generation of nuclear weapons to replace Trident. There was also considerable resistance from Labour MPs, and enough of them voted against the Trident replacement proposal to force Blair to rely on support from the Conservatives. By the end of March, Blair got his way: a replacement submarine, including missiles and warheads, and even that would be no less than 17 years in the making.

Cold War legacy

Since the end of the Cold War, the problem of the spread of nuclear weapons has become more complicated, not less. The legacy of the Cold War has played an important role. After the fall of the Berlin Wall and the collapse of the Soviet empire, the first challenge was to dismantle what Soviet premier Mikhail Gorbachev referred to as the 'infrastructure of fear' that had dominated global security relations during the Cold War, and Washington and Moscow declared the arms race over with the signing of the START Treaty in August 1991. Stopping it was one thing; reversing direction was quite another.

It is hard to find anyone who can offer a convincing argument as to why the United States and Russia both still need thousands of operational nuclear weapons in their stockpiles so many years after the end of the Cold War. Today, according to former Secretary of Defense Robert McNamara, the United States has deployed approximately 4,500 strategic offensive nuclear warheads and the Russians roughly 3,800. (The strategic forces of the UK, France, and China are considerably smaller, with 200 to 400 nuclear weapons in each state's arsenal; the newer nuclear states of India and Pakistan have fewer than 100 weapons each.) Of the 8,000 active or operational US warheads – each with the destructive power 20 times that of Hiroshima – 2,000 are on hair-trigger alert, ready to be launched on 15 minutes' warning. Moreover, the United States remains prepared to initiate the use of these weapons by the decision of one person, the president – against either a nuclear or non-nuclear enemy whenever the president believes that it is deemed in the national interest.

One of the most pressing concerns of security experts and policymakers in the early 1990s was to secure the weapons of the former USSR while that empire imploded. In 1991, the break-up of the Soviet Union left nuclear weapons in the former Soviet states of Ukraine, Belarus, and Kazakhstan. These newly independent states, each of which was 'born nuclear', were ultimately convinced to give up their inherited weapons, and all of those nuclear weapons were repatriated to Russia, but not without much anxiety. That the new states would simply give up these powerful bargaining chips was no foregone conclusion. The Nunn-Lugar programme, with considerable US funding to secure these weapons, aided in achieving a successful transfer. The sheer numbers of nuclear weapons even combined with this relatively modest dispersal illustrated the problem of command, control, and security in an environment of deteriorating military infrastructure. Whether a cash-strapped military complex might look to liquidate its assets or the compromising of security measures allowed theft, the threat to the international community was acute.

The problem seemed even more worrying with those weapons dispersed further afield. During the Cold War, both sides deployed tens of thousands of nuclear weapons and nuclear-capable delivery vehicles, well beyond their own borders in the name of forward defence and pre-positioning. The list of locations beyond the continental United States to which American nuclear weapons, both tactical and strategic, were dispersed is surprisingly long: Alaska, Canada, Greenland, Guam, Hawaii, Japan, Johnston Island, Kwajalein, Midway, Morocco, the Philippines, Puerto Rico, South Korea, Spain, Taiwan, Belgium, France, Greece, Italy, Netherlands, Turkey, the United Kingdom, and West Germany. In Europe alone, thousands of American nuclear weapons had been deployed since September 1954 in a constantly rotating inventory of obsolescence and replacement, peaking at approximately 7,300 in 1971.

The number of American nuclear weapons deployed overseas has been reduced markedly since the dissolution of the Soviet Union. In 1991, President George H.W. Bush ordered the withdrawal of all ground- and sea-based tactical nuclear weapons from their overseas bases. But the United States remains the only nation to continue locating land-based nuclear weapons beyond its own borders (other countries continue to deploy sea- and air-based weapons). The number of American nuclear weapons based in Europe remains at about 480.

Nuclear deterrence for the post-Cold War era

The break-up of the Soviet Union augured a new reality in which 'The prospect of a Soviet invasion into Western Europe, launched with little or no warning, was no longer a realistic threat.' Gorbachev shared the sentiment, describing it as a revolution in strategic thinking; no longer should the deterrent to war be the threat of war. 'Our next goal', he said, 'is to make full use of this breakthrough to make disarmament an irreversible process'.

By the time Bill Clinton assumed the presidency, the euphoria of the end of the Cold War was giving way to more sober analysis. It had become increasingly apparent that the problems associated with nuclear weapons had not actually faded away – they had simply been transformed. Rather than opening an era of global peace and security, the end of the Cold War paved the way for instability and the resurfacing of regional issues that had long been suppressed. Sarajevo, Kosovo, and Rwanda became household words.

Nevertheless, the Clinton administration pressed ahead with its efforts to align nuclear policy with new circumstances. In late 1993, it announced that the US government had adopted a new understanding of 'deterrence'. A wide-ranging and thorough 'Bottom Up Review', conducted by the Pentagon during 1993, identified a number of key threats to US national security.

Foremost among them was the increased threat of proliferation of nuclear weapons and other weapons of mass destruction. The new 'deterrence', therefore, would be aimed at deterring not only the threat to use nuclear weapons but also the acquisition of atomic technology and materials. By employing significant military and economic disincentives, the administration hoped to neutralize some of the chief threats to stability such as North Korea, Iraq, and Libya.

But the central thrust of US nuclear policy remained the potential of a resurgent Russia. In keeping with its redefinition of 'deterrence', the Clinton administration announced in September 1994 that it was adopting a new nuclear doctrine. The doctrine of mutual assured destruction, or MAD, was to be replaced with a policy of mutual assured safety, aimed primarily at the Russian heartland. This served a dual purpose: first, to provide leadership for continuing reductions in nuclear weapons, and, second, and more critically, to provide a hedge against a reversal of the reform process in Russia. Although it remained unlikely that Russia's weak economy could rebuild a conventional force of the magnitude that it had maintained during the Cold War, US defence planners speculated that nuclear weapons might offer an attractive, cheaper option to a new generation of Russian leaders.

In November 1997, Clinton issued a Presidential Decision Directive describing in general terms the purposes of US nuclear weapons while providing broad guidance for developing operational plans. It was the first such presidential directive on the actual employment of nuclear weapons since the Carter administration. It was notable in that Washington finally abandoned the Cold War tenet that it must be prepared to fight a protracted nuclear war. The directive also noted that strategic nuclear weapons would play a smaller role in the US security posture than at any other point during the second half of the 20th century, but that they were still a vital part of US efforts as a hedge against an uncertain future. But for those that believed that deterrence was a thing of the past, Clinton's directive served as a sharp reminder that not much had changed. In words still ringing from those at the height of the Cold War, the Clinton administration declared:

> Deterrence is predicated on ensuring that potential adversaries accept that any use of nuclear weapons against the United States or its allies would not succeed ... A wide range of nuclear retaliatory options are required to ensure that the United States is not left with an all-or-nothing response ... The United States will retain sufficient ambiguity of use that an adversary could never be sure that the United States would not launch a counter-attack before the adversary's weapons arrive.

At the same time, Aspin's successor, Secretary of Defense William Cohen, wondered aloud whether a smaller nuclear force made it a more attractive target and deliberately cultivated the ambiguity concept upon which deterrence rested.

With transition to a coherent post-Cold War posture incomplete, the United States publicly considers Moscow an ally, while Pentagon war-game scenarios involving Moscow as the primary enemy continue. For its part, Russia maintains a nuclear force of considerable size, ostensibly to make up for the deterioration of its conventional capabilities.

Effectiveness of non-proliferation efforts

Non-proliferation efforts in recent years have enjoyed mixed results. On the one hand, nuclear stockpiles have been reduced markedly, with some of that fissile material being converted to peaceful purposes by blending down bomb-grade plutonium and uranium to lower-grade versions more suitable for nuclear power production. 'One out of every ten light bulbs in the United States is powered by a former Soviet bomb', boasted Ambassador Linton Brooks, administrator of the US National Nuclear Security

Administration. On the other hand, the risk of nuclear weapons or fissile materials falling into the wrong hands seems greater than ever.

As of September 2005, there had been 220 cases of nuclear smuggling confirmed by the International Atomic Energy Agency since 1993. Eighteen of those cases involved highly enriched uranium. There are ongoing fears about Russian accountability for small, suitcase-sized bombs after former Russian national security adviser Alexander Lebed made a startling public claim in 1997 that up to 100 of those bombs were unaccounted for. Originally envisaged for use by spies behind enemy lines for sabotage and demolition in the event of war, the weapons were designed to be highly portable, self-contained, and possibly with short-cuts in their arming and detonation procedures. Put another way, they are a terrorist's dream. '[M]ore than a hundred weapons out of the supposed number of 250 are not under the control of the armed forces of Russia', Lebed said in a September 1997 interview on the American television programme *60 Minutes*. 'I don't know their location. I don't know whether they have been destroyed or whether they are stored or whether they've been sold or stolen, I don't know.' Lebed's claims have been the subject of vigorous debate.

The issue is more than historical curiosity. On 11 October 2001, just one month after terrorists struck in New York and Washington, CIA Director George Tenet briefed President Bush that, according to a CIA source, Al Qaeda had stolen a small nuclear bomb from the Russian arsenal. That bomb, according to the source, was then in New York City. The intelligence proved false. Nonetheless, thefts of nuclear-usable material and attempts to steal nuclear weapons were no longer in the realm of the hypothetical, but a proven, recurring fact of international life. According to Graham Allison, 'Thousands of weapons and tens of thousands of potential weapons (softball-size lumps of highly enriched uranium and plutonium) remain today in unsecured storage facilities in Russia, vulnerable to theft by determined criminals who could then sell them to terrorists.' In the years since the end of the Cold War, there have been numerous cases of theft of nuclear materials in which the thieves were captured, sometimes in Russia, on other occasions in the Czech Republic, Germany, and elsewhere.

There is also the problem of the spread of nuclear weapons to weak or failing states. Illustrating the immediacy of the problem was the case of the international trafficking of atomic technology and materials set up by Pakistani atomic scientist Dr A. Q. Khan. It amounted to a 'one-stop shopping network for nuclear weapons'. By all accounts, Khan's operation was a highly sophisticated supply and production network spreading from Pakistan to Libya, North Korea, Iran, Malaysia, and elsewhere. Shutting it down had immediate, flow-on effects. Khan's network had played a crucial role in Libya's nuclear ambitions. Within months of the network being shut down in 2004, Libya had renounced its nuclear

7. Supporters in Pakistan rallying with posters of Dr A. Q. Khan, whom they viewed as the 'Father of the Islamic Bomb'

programme, allowed international inspectors into the country, and given up much of the supporting technology.

It was a proliferation breakthrough of unusual drama. It was also sobering: the network was sophisticated, effective, and had operated undetected for several years. Though A. Q. Khan and his known cohorts are out of business, there is still the great unanswered question: Who else might have access to the nuclear technology he and his network proliferated? We simply don't know, according to London strategic studies think-tank chief, John Chipman, as:

> Pakistan has never made public Khan's confession, the details of its investigation into the network, including who was arrested and who was simply detained 'for debriefing', the charges and laws under which Khan's associates were detained, the grounds for their release, or the identities of those who were put under a form of continued 'house arrest'.

Pakistan has stopped providing information on the official grounds that the Khan case is closed. In addition, most of Khan's foreign accomplices remain free and only three have been convicted and imprisoned. The upshot is the real concern that the international framework of export controls still contains serious gaps that could well be exploited by a network similar to that of Khan.

What do we know, then? We do know that the dismantling of the A. Q. Khan network had the appearance of a notable success of aggressive non-proliferation efforts and putatively led directly to tangible counter-proliferation progress in compelling Libya to abandon its nuclear ambitions and its advanced weapons programmes. At first glance, the Libyan case seemed a model of successful deterrence, but first appearances proved deceptive. Encouraged by the coincidence of timing with the invasion of Iraq and the heated domestic political environment, early news reports of Libya's decision to end its nuclear ambitions implied that deterrence had played a key role. Perhaps Colonel Qadafi had feared that Libya might face the same fate as Saddam's Iraq. The later exposure of Libya's reliance on Khan's network put events into a better perspective. While Qadafi might have been deterred to some extent, it was probably not the primary driving force behind Tripoli's decision. Libya had simply been caught red-handed, flaunting international rules against the trafficking of nuclear technology and materials. Confronted with undeniable evidence of its wrongdoing and deprived of its principal source for continuing the nuclear programme, it probably saw more political advantage in 'confessing' and renouncing nuclear weapons rather than in denying reality. Qadafi was proved right.

Another troubling complication in controlling proliferation is the blurred line between civilian atomic energy programmes and weapons programmes. Much effort in recent years has been directed towards establishing clear demarcation lines between them, but it always remains possible for a civilian atomic energy programme to migrate to a nuclear weapons programme. Civilian atomic energy programmes build expertise, contribute technology, and produce material. It is a characteristic recently exploited by two of the three countries President Bush notoriously identified as part of 'an axis of evil'. Iran has long insisted that its nuclear ambitions lie only in civilian atomic energy reactors; the international community, including the International Atomic Energy Agency, remains unpersuaded. Teheran's claim that is has a 'peaceful' right to acquire all it needs to come within range of having a bomb served as a reminder of what the NPT was meant to avoid. Iran, for whatever reason, continues to reject international demands to suspend its uranium enrichment programme.

By agreements concluded with the Clinton administration, North Korea was putatively allowed to maintain a strictly civilian atomic energy programme. Clearly, North Korea was intent on using its energy reactors to enrich uranium, the key ingredient required for an atomic weapon. But problems with North Korea over nuclear proliferation were nothing new. The regime started building nuclear reactors in the 1960s and did not join the NPT until 1985, while the signing of a safeguards agreement that would permit the IAEA inspections of its nuclear programme was postponed until 1992. When the overdue inspections suggested that the North Koreans were hiding nuclear material, the Democratic People's Republic of Korea became the first country to announce its withdrawal from the NPT, dramatically suspended one day before it became effective. Then came the period under the Agreed Framework in 1994, which, for a number of reasons, collapsed in 2002. The Agreed Framework, worked out by the Clinton administration, required the US both to help North Korea to acquire modern, light water reactors that would produce energy but not weapons and to move towards normal relations. Neither of these happened, as Clinton's successor pushed for the so-called 'six-party talks' on North Korea in which the two Koreas, China, Russia, Japan, and the United States were jointly to reach a solution with Kim Il Sung's Stalinist-style regime.

On 9 October 2006, North Korea exploded a plutonium bomb in a tunnel at a place called Punggye in the far north of the country, becoming the ninth country in history – and arguably the most unstable and dangerous – to proclaim that it had joined the club of nuclear weapons states. Why would North Korea want to acquire nuclear weapons – defence, offence, diplomatic bargaining chip? No one was quite sure. What to do about it was equally problematical. The normally sober *New York Times* editorialized that this was going to be a problem as North Korea 'is too erratic, too brutal, and too willing to sell what it has built to have a nuclear bomb'. The shortage of information on the generally reclusive North Korean nuclear programme remains a serious issue for the international community, especially when this nation has repeatedly demonstrated antagonistic security policies. The possibility of some form of military conflict on the Korean peninsula in the years ahead remains high, as it seems highly probable that North Korea would seriously contemplate using nuclear weapons in combat. The North Korean nuclear problem will not go away despite Pyongyang's repeated counter-proposal to rescind its nuclear programme in exchange for energy and diplomatic concessions. At this juncture, it is hard to tell exactly what, if anything, it would take for North Korea to give up its nuclear arsenal.

Finally, there is the problem of the proliferation of weapons states in South Asia. Efforts to roll back the India-Pakistan nuclear arms race have been spectacularly unsuccessful. Admittedly, the problem had been handled very differently from the Libyan case. India joined the nuclear club with a successful test on 18 May 1974, having begun its programme in response to the border clash with China in November 1962, with China developing its own bomb two years later. Since then, India maintained a 'dual front' approach to its defence planning, with Pakistan and China clearly in its sights. But it is the India-Pakistan front that has been the cause of intense global concern since things heated up considerably in mid-1998. The two countries have had a marked history of conflict during the relatively short life of the Pakistani nation. It is a rivalry fuelled by many cultural and security issues, and it has a ready-made flashpoint in the contested territory of Jammu and Kashmir.

Since 1947, when Pakistan was carved off India by the British, serious military conflict has broken out between the two sides at least four times. Each time India has won. The injection of nuclear weapons into that volatile mix has naturally led to widespread concern. In May 1998, India tested five nuclear weapons. Before the month was out, Pakistan had hastily responded with six nuclear tests of its own. Each side engaged in sabre-rattling rhetoric and tension has built up on several occasions since, most notably in brinkmanship of dual mobilizations in 2002. The tests

8. An Indian nuclear test site in Rajasthan, May 1998

provoked widespread international condemnation aimed at both parties.

Whether nuclear weapons stabilize or destabilize the India-Pakistan rivalry remains a controversial question. Deterrence optimists argue that the risks of even a small-scale nuclear exchange on the subcontinent, where the urban environments would almost certainly lead to millions of deaths, should force each side back from the brink. Former Indian minister of external affairs Jaswant Singh fell in that camp, adding that those who were condemning India's nuclear policies loudest were engaging in what amounted to 'nuclear apartheid'. 'If deterrence works in the West – as it so obviously appears to', he argued, 'by what reasoning will it not work in India?' The Pakistani leadership professed similar views: a nuclear conflict would surely have no victor. In South Asia, nuclear deterrence may, however, usher in an era of durable peace between Pakistan and India, providing the requisite incentives for resolving all outstanding issues, especially Jammu and Kashmir. This is the optimistic view. Deterrence pessimists argue, however, that such a view places far too much trust in the organizational integrity of the respective military establishments. Could either side actually control the escalation of a crisis even if they wanted to? Many security experts fear not.

The nuclear experience of recent years suggests that the underlying approach of creating rigorous international norms and inspection supervisory regimes remains the best and most effective way of controlling nuclear threats. Mohamed El Baradei, director general of the International Atomic Energy Agency and winner of the 2005 Nobel Peace Prize, holds that 'We cannot respond to these threats by building more walls, developing bigger weapons or dispatching more troops. These threats require primarily multinational cooperation.' The IAEA works with the atomic programmes in more than 100 countries. El Baradei estimates that as many as 49 nations know how to make nuclear weapons and warns that global tension could well push some over the line. Still, the situation is not as bad as John F. Kennedy worried about in 1963 when he predicted that there could be well over 15 or 20 nuclear powers by end of the decade. Interestingly, his concern was not that developing nations would acquire the bomb, but rather that advanced industrial economies would do so, particularly West Germany and Japan. Several European nations, including neutral Sweden, which was then developing plans to build 100 nuclear weapons to equip its armed forces, were already actively pursuing nuclear weapons programmes.

On the other side of the ledger, the G. W. Bush administration's policies had been informed by a robust scepticism of the actual effectiveness of international controls and have often emphasized more aggressive counter-proliferation efforts, turning its attention more and more to deterring the acquisition of atomic technology and materials, a policy initiated in the Clinton years. Bush revealed himself to be a deterrence pessimist of the first order. In justifying the invasion of Iraq, Bush declared: 'I acted because

I was not about to leave the security of the American people in the hands of a madman. I was not about to stand by and wait and trust in the sanity and restraint of Saddam Hussein.'

The invasion of Iraq in March 2003 was therefore presented mainly as an effort to destroy Iraqi weapons of mass destruction programmes, for fear that Saddam could not be deterred and, implicitly, that he might try to turn the tables on the United States and its allies. 'We don't want the smoking gun to be a mushroom cloud', then national security adviser Condoleezza Rice said in October 2002 in the lead-up to the war. As is well known, it turned out that Iraq had no weapons of mass destruction, particularly of the nuclear kind. Less well known, paradoxically, is that the invasion reinvigorated the very argument that inspection regimes such as the one imposed on Iraq during the 1990s could indeed be effective instruments in slowing or stopping the spread of nuclear weapons. Unfortunately, for the people of Iraq – and the Coalition of the Willing – Bush called Saddam's bluff.

The clarity of the Cold War world has given way to the ambiguities and uncertainties of a world where global security is threatened by regime collapse, nuclear terrorism, new nuclear weapons states and regional conflict, and pre-existing nuclear arsenals. The dangers inherent in such a mix are in themselves greatly magnified by easier access to nuclear technology, inadequately protected stockpiles of plutonium and highly enriched uranium, the growing availability of missiles worldwide (31 nations with ballistic missiles), black-market nuclear supply networks, and a trend towards acquisition of 'latent' nuclear weapons capabilities through the possession of the entire nuclear fuel cycle. The results are clear: of all the potential threats to the global community today (including global warming), nuclear weapons, the most deadly weapon ever invented – and really the only true weapon of mass destruction – probably pose the greatest risk. Indeed, the bomb still matters.

References and further reading

In addition to the giants on whose shoulders I have stood for more than 30 years and who are recognized in the text and bibliography that follows, I should like to thank the many archivists and librarians in the United States, Australia, and the United Kingdom who are all too often taken for granted. I should also like to thank my former students Jason Flanagan and Jacqui Bird for their thoughtful analyses of the career of J. Robert Oppenheimer and the role of atomic scientists in the making of nuclear weapons, respectively. Needless to say, there is a vast literature on various aspects of the politics of nuclear weaponry and the problems and prospects of dealing with nuclear weapons. The publications listed below represent the tip of that iceberg and include the most important studies in English. Constraints of space have made it necessary to omit many excellent and important works in the field.

Chapter 1

The best place to begin the study of nuclear weapons is the pages of the *Bulletin of Atomic Scientists*, founded in 1945 as a newsletter distributed among nuclear physicists concerned by the possibility of nuclear war; for 60 years the *Bulletin*'s Doomsday Clock has followed the rise and fall of nuclear tensions. For a discussion of the far-reaching effects of nuclear weapons, including the mass fire caused by firestorms, see Lynn Eden, *Whole World on Fire: Organizations, Knowledge, and Nuclear Weapons Devastation* (Cornell University Press, 2004). The best introduction to the threat posed by nuclear terrorists is Graham Allison, *Nuclear Terrorism: The Ultimate Preventable Catastrophe* (Times Books, 2004); also useful are Scott D. Sagan and Kenneth N. Waltz, *The Spread of Nuclear Weapons: A Debate Renewed* (W. W. Norton, 2003) and Joseph Cirincione, Jon Wolfstahl, and Miriam Rajkumar, *Deadly Arsenals: Nuclear, Biological and Chemical Threats* (Carnegie Endowment for International Peace, 2005).

Chapter 2

The Einstein letter together with FDR's reply is found in Vincent C. Jones, *Manhattan: The Army and the Atomic Bomb* (US Government Printing Office, 1985). A good introduction to the Einstein story, taking into account all the latest discoveries of letters and organized in a conventional chronological format, is Walter Isaacson, *Einstein: His Life and Universe* (Simon and Schuster, 2007). For details on the German research effort, see Richard Rhodes, *The Making of the Atomic Bomb* (Simon and Schuster, 1986); McGeorge Bundy, *Danger and Survival: Choices about the Bomb in the First Fifty Years* (Random House, 1988); Mark Walker, *German National Socialism and the Quest for Nuclear Power, 1939–1949* (Cambridge University Press, 1989); and Jeffey T. Richelson, *Spying on the Bomb: American Nuclear Intelligence from Nazi Germany to Iran and North Korea* (Norton, 2006). The best introduction to the making of the atomic bomb is still Henry D. Smyth, *A General Account of the Development of Methods of Using Atomic Energy for Military Purposes under the Auspices of the United States Government, 1940–1945* (US Government Printing Office, 1945).

For the role of the atomic scientists, see Robert Jungk, *Brighter Than a Thousand Suns: The Moral and Political History of the Atomic Scientists* (Victor Gollancz, 1958); Robert Gilpin, *American Scientists and Nuclear Weapons Policy* (Princeton University Press, 1962); and Gregg Herken, *Brotherhood of the Bomb: The Tangled Lives and Loyalties of Robert Oppenheimer, Ernest Lawrence, Edward Teller* (Henry Holt, 2002). Also see Jacqueline Bird's related essay in *The Politics of Nuclear Weaponry*, ed. Richard Dean Burns and Joseph M. Siracusa (Regina Books, 2007).

The 'atomic diplomacy' debate may be followed in Gar Alperovitz, *The Decision to Use the Atomic Bomb and the Architecture of an American Debate* (Harper Collins, 1995); Robert James Maddox, *Weapons for Victory: The Hiroshima Decision Fifty Years Later* (University of Missouri Press, 1995); and, most recently, Wilson D. Miscamble, *From Roosevelt to Truman: Potsdam, Hiroshima, and the Cold War* (Cambridge University Press, 2007). For a useful distillation of the vast literature on this subject, see J. Samuel Walker, *Prompt and Utter Destruction: Truman and the Use of Atomic Bombs against Japan* (University of North Carolina Press, 1997).

For the impact of wartime bombing of civilians, see Jorg Friedich, *Fire: The Bombing of Germany, 1940–45* (Columbia University Press, 2007), and the incomparable John Hersey, *Hiroshima* (Penguin, 1946). The George Orwell quote is found in *Orwell in Tribune: 'As I Please' and Other Writings, 1943–7*, compiled and edited by Paul Anderson (Politioco's, 2007).

Chapter 3

The Baruch Plan and the Gromyko proposal are found in Joseph M. Siracusa, *The American Diplomatic Revolution: A Documentary History of the Cold War, 1941–1947* (Holt, Rinehart and Winston, 1976). For a detailed treatment of the Baruch Plan, which contains a fair amount of primary source material, see Leneice N. Wu's essay in Richard Dean Burns (ed.), *Encyclopaedia of Arms Control and Disarmament* (3 vols, Charles Scribner's Sons, 1993), and Richard G. Hewlett and Oscar E. Anderson, Jr, *A History of the United States*

Atomic Energy Commission, vol. 1, *The New World, 1939/1946* (University of Pennsylvania, 1962).

The best historical assessments include Barton J. Bernstein, 'The Quest for Security: American Foreign Policy and International Control of Atomic Energy', *Journal of American History* 60 (March 1974), 1003–44; and Larry Gerber, 'The Baruch Plan and the Origins of the Cold War', *Diplomatic History* 6 (Winter 1982), 69–95. The Bush quote is found in the introduction of Thomas C. Reed's *At the Abyss: An Insider's History of the Cold War* (Ballantine Books, 2004).

Chapter 4

Portions of this chapter have been adapted from my recent study, with David G. Coleman, *Real-World Nuclear Deterrence: The Making of International Strategy* (Praeger Security International, 2006). The famous NSC 68 document is found in Joseph M. Siracusa, *Into the Dark House: American Diplomacy and the Ideological Origins of the Cold War* (Regina Books, 1998).

For the historical context of these years, see Paul Boyer, *By the Bomb's Early Light: American Thought and Culture at the Dawn of the Atomic Age* (North Carolina Press, 1994); Michael Mandelbaum, *The Nuclear Revolution: International Politics before and after Hiroshima* (Cambridge University Press, 1981); and Michael J. Hogan, *A Cross of Iron: Harry S. Truman and the Origins of the National Security States, 1945–1954* (Cambridge University Press, 1998).

Also useful are Gregg Herken, *The Winning Weapon: The Atomic Bomb in the Cold War, 1945–1950* (Knopf, 1980); Margaret Gowing, *Independence and Deterrence: Britain and Atomic Energy, 1945–1952* (Macmillan, 1974); and John Lewis Gaddis et al. (eds) *Cold War Statesmen Confront the Bomb* (Oxford University Press, 1999).

The Soviet side of this story is told ably in David Holloway, *Stalin and the Bomb: The Soviet Union and Atomic Energy, 1939–1956* (Yale University Press, 1994); and Vojtech Mastny, *The Cold War and Soviet Insecurity: The Stalin Years* (Oxford University Press, 1996).

The growth of the global anti-nuclear campaign, together with the forces, personalities, and events that moulded it, is told in Lawrence S. Wittner's incomparable multi-volume study, *The Struggle against the Bomb* (Stanford University Press, 1993–).

Chapter 5

Indispensable are three works by Raymond L. Garthoff: *Deterrence and the Revolution in Soviet Military Doctrine* (Brookings Institution, 1990), *Soviet Strategy in the Nuclear Age* (rev. edn, Praeger, 1962), and *Détente and Confrontation: American Soviet Relations from Nixon to Reagan* (Brookings Institution, 1985). In this same category I also include Lawrence Freedman's *The Evolution of Nuclear Strategy*, 3rd edn (Palgrave Macmillan, 2003) and *Deterrence* (Polity, 2004).

Still useful on nuclear doctrine are Thomas C. Schelling, *Arms and Influence* (Yale University Press, 1966), and Glenn H. Snyder, *Deterrence and Defence* (Princeton University Press, 1961).

Of the several accounts of the Cuban Missile Crisis, Graham Allison and Philip Zelikow's *Essence of Decision: Explaining the Cuban Missile Crisis*, 2nd edn (Longman, 1999) is the standard account. Alexandr Fursenko and Timothy Naftali, *'One Hell of a Gamble': Khrushchev, Castro and Kennedy, 1958–1964, Secret History of the Cuban Missile Crisis* (W. W. Norton, 1997), had unprecedented access to the former Soviet archives, while Ernest R. May and Philip Zelikow, *The Kennedy Tapes: Inside the White House during the Cuban Missile Crisis* (Belknap Press, 1997), provides transcripts of most of the audio recordings JFK secretly made during the episode.

The treaty milestones of these years are covered in Joseph M. Siracusa and David G. Coleman, *Depression to Cold War: A History of America from Herbert Hoover to Ronald Reagan* (Praeger, 2002), and Richard Dean Burns (ed.), *Encyclopaedia of Arms Control and Disarmament* (3 vols, Charles Scribner's sons, 1993).

Arms control efforts to limit the potential threat of strategic weaponry may be found in McGeorge Bundy, *Danger and Survival*; J. P. G. Freeman, *Britain's Nuclear Arms Control Policy in the Context of Anglo-American Relations, 1957–68* (St Martin's Press, 1986); Martin Goldstein, *Arms Control and Military Preparedness from Truman to Bush* (Peter Lang, 1993); and Robin Ranger, *Arms and Politics, 1958–1978: Arms Control in a Changing Political Context* (Gage, 1979). Kennedy's creation of the Arms Control and Disarmament Agency is described by Duncan L. Clarke, *Politics of Arms Control: The Role and Effectiveness of the Arms Control and Disarmament Agency* (Free Press, 1979).

The debate over nuclear testing and negotiation of the limited test ban treaty are detailed in Robert Divine, *Blowing on the Wind: The Nuclear Test Ban Debate, 1954–1960* (Oxford University Press, 1978); Glenn Seaborg, *Kennedy, Khrushchev and the Test Ban* (University of California Press, 1981); Kendrick Oliver, *Kennedy, Macmillan, and the Nuclear Test-Ban Treaty* (St Martin's Press, 1998); and William R. Cleave and S. T. Cohen, *Nuclear Weapons, Policies, and the Test Ban Issues* (Praeger, 1987).

For the Reagan years and arms control, see Strobe Talbott, *Deadly Gambits: The Reagan Administration and the Stalemate in Nuclear Arms Control* (Knopf, 1984); Kenneth L. Adelman, *The Great Universal Embrace: Arms Summitry, a Skeptic's Account* (Simon and Schuster, 1989); and Keith L. Shimko, *Images and Arms Control: Perceptions of the Soviet Union in the Reagan Administration* (University of Michigan Press, 1991).

Also useful are Alexander L. George and Richard Smoke, *Deterrence in American Foreign Policy: Theory and Practice* (Columbia University Press, 1974); Fred Kaplan, *The Wizards of Armageddon* (Simon and Schuster, 1983); and Marc Trachtenberg, *History and Strategy* (Princeton University Press, 1991).

Chapter 6

Overviews include Richard Dean Burns and Lester H. Brune, *The Quest for Missile Defenses, 1944–2003* (Regina Books, 2004); Ashton B. Carter and David N. Schwartz (eds), *Ballistic Missile Defense* (Brookings Institution, 1984); and David B. H. Denoon, *Ballistic Missile Defense in the Post-Cold War Era* (Westview, 1995). For Soviet/Russian developments, see Pavel Podvig (ed.), *Russian Strategic Nuclear Forces* (MIT Press, 2001) and Steven J. Zaloga, *The Kremlin's Nuclear Sword: The Rise and Fall of Russia's Strategic Nuclear Forces, 1945–2000* (Smithsonian Institution Press, 2002).

The 1968 debates over deployment are covered in Edward R. Jayne, *The ABM Debate: Strategic Defense and National Security* (Center for Strategic Studies, 1969); Abram Chayes and Jerome Wiesner (eds), *ABM: An Evaluation of the Decision to Deploy an Antiballistic Missile System* (Harper and Row, 1969); and Ernest J. Yanarella, *The Missile Defense Controversy: Strategy, Technology, and Politics, 1955–1972* (University Press of Kentucky, 1977).

For the Reagan administration's efforts to reinterpret the ABM treaty, see Raymond L. Garthoff, *Policy Versus the Law: The Reinterpretation of the ABM Treaty* (Brookings Institution Press, 1987). For Reagan's initiative, consult William L. Broad, *Teller's War: The Top Secret Story Behind the Star Wars' Deception* (Simon and Schuster, 1992) and Frances Fitzgerald, *Way Out There in the Blue: Reagan, Star Wars and the End of the Cold War* (Simon and Schuster, 2000).

Chapter 7

In addition to the works noted in Chapter 1, see Stephen J. Cimbala, *Nuclear Strategy in the Twenty-First Century* (Praeger, 2000).

The importance of the Nuclear Non-Proliferation Treaty is discussed in Ted Greenwood, Harold A. Feiveson, and Theodore A. Taylor, *Nuclear Proliferation: Motivations, Capabilities and Strategies for Control* (McGraw-Hill, 1977); Michael P. Fry, Patrick Keatinge, and Joseph Rotblat (eds), *Nuclear Non-Proliferation and the Non-Proliferation Treaty* (Springer-Verlag, 1990); David Fischer, *Stopping the Spread of Nuclear Weapons: The Past and the Prospects* (Taylor and Francis, 1992); and T. V. Paul, *Power Versus Prudence: Why Nations Forgo Nuclear Weapons* (McGill-Queens University Press, 2000).

For the rise and fall of Dr A. Q. Khan and his nuclear black market, see William Langewiesche, *The Atomic Bazaar: The Rise of the Nuclear Poor* (Farrar, Straus and Giroux, 2007) and *Nuclear Black Markets: Pakistan, A. Q. Khan and the Rise of Proliferation Networks* (International Institute for Strategic Studies, London, 2007).

Recent studies of how not to deal with North Korea are Marion V. Creekmore, Jr, *A Moment of Crisis: Jimmy Carter, the Power of a Peacemaker, and North Korea's Nuclear Ambitions* (Public Affairs, 2007); Gordon D. Chang, *Nuclear Showdown: North Korea Takes on the World* (Random House, 2007); and Jasper Becker, *Rogue Regime: Kim Jong Il and the Looming Threat of North Korea* (Oxford University Press, 2007).

For the problems and prospects of the proliferation of nuclear weapons states in South Asia, see Devin T. Hagerty, *The Consequences of Nuclear Proliferation: Lessons from South Asia* (MIT Press, 1998); George Perkovich, *India's Nuclear Bomb: The Impact on Global Proliferation* (University of California Press, 1999); and K. K. Pathak,

Nuclear Policy of India: A Third World Perspective (Gitanjali Prakashan, 1980).

For an account of nuclear 'know-how' gone astray, consult John McPhee, *The Curve of Binding Energy* (Farrar, Straus and Giroux, 1974). And to understand how easy it would be for a terrorist organization to assemble an atomic bomb, see Peter D. Zimmerman and Jeffrey G. Lewis, 'The Bomb in the Backyard', *Foreign Policy* (November–December 2006), 33–9.

Index

D

E

F

G

H

I

J

K

Index

W

Visit the
VERY SHORT
INTRODUCTIONS
Web site

www.oup.co.uk/vsi

➤ **Information** about all published titles

➤ News of **forthcoming books**

➤ **Extracts** from the books, including titles not yet published

➤ **Reviews** and views

➤ **Links** to other **web sites** and main OUP web page

➤ Information about **VSIs in translation**

➤ **Contact** the editors

➤ **Order** other **VSIs** on-line